BUILT

DIFFERENT

Harrison House

Shippensburg, PA

BUILT

DIFFERENT

90 DAYS TO BECOMING ALL
GOD WANTS YOU TO BE

GABE POIROT

Published by Harrison House Publishers
Shippensburg, PA 17257

ISBN 13 TP: 978-1-6803-1882-1

ISBN 13 eBook: 978-1-6803-1883-8

ISBN 13 HC: 978-1-6803-1884-5

For Worldwide Distribution, Printed in the U.S.A.

1 2 3 4 5 6 7 8 / 27 26 25 24 23 22

CONTENTS

DAY 1

BUILT DIFFERENT

But as many as received Him, to them He gave
the right to become children of God, to those
who believe in His name (John 1:12 NKJV).

I t is safe to say that Bronny James has grown up a little different than the rest of the world. Everything from his original DNA to his daily lifestyle is altered because of his father, Lebron James, who is an NBA legend who has won four NBA championships. Bronny James, because of his family, is *built different* for basketball. While I am sure he has worked hard and invested into his skills, he already had an advantage being the son of one of the greatest basketball players of all time.

We also have an advantage. The Bible says, "But as many as received Him [Jesus], to them He gave the right to become children of God, to those who believe in His name" (John 1:12 NKJV). Before anything else, you must understand that you are a *child of God*. If you have not yet been born again, or if you question your salvation, the Bible says clearly:

> *If you confess with your mouth the Lord Jesus*
> *and believe in your heart that God has raised*
> *Him from the dead, you will be saved. For with*
> *the heart one believes unto righteousness, and*

with the mouth confession is made unto salvation (Romans 10:9 NKJV).

No one gets to choose their birth parents, but everyone has a choice about whether or not they will accept God as their Father. The way to be sure of your salvation and enter into Father God's family is to believe in His Son, Jesus. Jesus said, in John 3:16, "For God so loved the world that he gave his one and only Son, that whoever believes in him shall not perish but have eternal life." To receive Him, pray the declaration below out loud with all of your heart.

DECLARATION:

Jesus, I believe that You died on the cross. You took my place and bore my sin. And three days later, You rose again. I repent of my sins, and I place my faith in You. Jesus, You are the Lord of my life. Thank You for saving me. I thank You that You have forgiven me. I am born again. I am in the family of God. I'm built different, because You, Jesus, are built different. Amen.

The truth is, when you place your faith in Christ, you truly become *built different*. You may not feel like it at all times, but it is the truth. Who you are on the inside has now been created brand new. Your past sins, mistakes, and failures are washed away. God doesn't see you through your sin. He sees you through the blood of Jesus Christ. Look at yourself in the mirror today and speak over yourself: *I am a new creation in Christ. Jesus lives in me. My past is gone.*

Scripture Reading: John 1

GOD DOESN'T CREATE USED ANDROIDS

*Therefore, if anyone is in Christ, he is a new creation;
old things have passed away; behold, all things
have become new* (2 Corinthians 5:17 NKJV).

I apologize to all my Android users out there. The first day of our devotional might not apply to you, because the blood of Jesus might not be thick enough to cover your sin of owning that atrocious phone. All jokes and sarcasm aside—think back to the day you first got your new phone. (Picture it as an iPhone.) When you opened up that package and breathed in that fresh new iPhone smell, did you ever question that phone's past? Did you think to yourself, *Where was this before? Did it have any problems?* If you have common sense, you won't question anything about the phone, because you know that it is *brand new*. Now again, if you have an Android, this example won't apply, because you never know if they are new or used.

My point is, there is a big difference between a refurbished or used iPhone and a brand-new iPhone. When something is just refurbished or used and then cleaned up, you will still have doubts. But when a phone is fresh out of the factory and brand spankin' new, it is *built different*.

The Bible says, "Therefore, if anyone is in Christ, he is a new creation; old things have passed away; behold, all things have become new" (2 Cor. 5:17 NKJV). When you decided to place your faith in Christ, God did not make a refurbished Android. He did not just clean you up. The blood of Jesus does not "improve" you. Your inner person, your very DNA, who you really are, has been made *brand new*. Just like you would never question a brand-new iPhone, it is time you stop doubting yourself because of your past mistakes. Choose to believe that God's Word is telling the truth concerning your place in Christ. Just as babies are born after their parents' DNA and likeness, so too you have the likeness of Father God.

Now, the reality is that you will not always feel brand new. There will be many times in your walk with God that you feel like your old self. You will have bad feelings and memories and shame and guilt that try to overtake you, but choose instead to let this be your stand. Choose to believe that you are indeed a new creation and your past mistakes and failures have been completely *forgiven and washed*.

DECLARATION:

I am a new creation in Christ Jesus. I am forgiven. I am washed in the blood of Jesus. My past is gone. There is no shame in me. There is no guilt in me. God sees me through the lens of the blood of Jesus. God finds no fault in me. God is not mad at me. I am not a failure.

Scripture Reading: 2 Corinthians 5

DAY 3

THE JOY OF JESUS

Do not be drunk with wine, in which is dissipation;
but be filled with the Spirit (Ephesians 5:18 NKJV).

Recently, I was hanging out in the hot tub outside my apartment when some people started to gather around. It was around 1 a.m. and approximately twenty young men and women were chilling and smoking dope and drinking. Now some people may question why I stayed, being a Christian, instead of just heading out. Well, here is the thing: (1) I was at the hot tub first, so I am not going to just finish with my time before I'm ready, and (2) the last time I checked, the Jesus that is inside of me is greater than the world around me. Now I am not saying this means you should go hang around friends who smoke and drink. I am just saying that, for this example, my butt was staying in that hot tub.

As they gathered around, they asked if I wanted to smoke. Instead of condemning them and telling them about how much God hated them, I chose to make friends. I went to their level and talked with them about rap and made some jokes. I told them, "I don't wanna take a hit, because I have the free stuff." They couldn't believe what I said. A lot of Christians, when it comes to drugs or alcohol, like to just say, "No, I do not do that." But actually, the Bible says,

Do not be drunk with wine, in which is dissipation; but be filled with the Spirit, speaking to one another in psalms and hymns and spiritual songs, singing and making melody in your heart to the Lord (Ephesians 5:18–19 NKJV).

What that means is that God has called us to get high every single day—high on the Holy Spirit. Tomorrow, I will tell you the crazy ending to that night in the hot tub, but before we close today, I want you to start changing your mind when it comes to how you live for God. *God is not boring. Jesus is not dull.* As Christians, we are actually called to live a life *high on the Holy Spirit.* We should be the most fun, full of joy, full of life young people on the planet. It is time the world looks at the church in a *jealous way*, wanting the joy that we carry. God does not want you to put away your joy and happiness in order to follow Him. The devil perverted fun and made sin look like it was better than God's way, but the devil actually cannot create anything. God was the one who created fun and good times.

DECLARATION:

Father God, thank You for giving me breath today. Thank You for giving the Holy Spirit to me. I will not use drugs or get drunk on alcohol. Thank You for giving me the chance to be high on the Holy Spirit every single day. I have the joy of the Lord. Teach me how to have fun. Show me how I can shine bright to everyone around me.

Scripture Reading: Ephesians 5

DAY 4

HOT TUBBIN' WITH JESUS

You are the light of the world...

(Matthew 5:14 NKJV).

Now back to the hot tub situation. The craziest thing happened that night. Now, I'll be honest with you: I don't really know most secular songs. It seems like most secular music is just boppin' out to money, sex, and fame. It is very worldly and not fruitful to listen to, but everyone at the hot tub was vibing out to the music. As I talked with a group of guys, they started feeling more comfortable around me. I asked them a ton of questions and showed that I cared for them. Also, I made sure not to judge them, and I didn't call the apartment manager.

As this was going on, I found myself recognizing the beat to a song they were playing. Turns out it was "Our God Is Greater" by Chris Tomlin! All of a sudden these worldly people were vibing out to a worship song. They pointed at me and said, "This one's for you, free stuff." While they didn't all get on their knees and repent before God, the truth is that they were all impacted by the love of God that night. The Bible says, in 1 Corinthians 3:6–7,

> *I planted the seed, Apollos watered it, but God has been making it grow. So neither the one*

who plants nor the one who waters is anything, but only God, who makes things grow.

I need you to understand and always remember what it says in 1 John 4:4: "You are of God, little children, and have overcome them, because He who is in you is greater than he who is in the world" (NKJV). God always wants you to influence the world around you instead of the world changing you. We are called to be light in a dark world. Jesus said,

> *You are the light of the world. A city that is set on a hill cannot be hidden. Nor do they light a lamp and put it under a basket, but on a lampstand, and it gives light to all who are in the house. Let your light so shine before men, that they may see your good works and glorify your Father in heaven* (Matthew 5:14 NKJV).

God uses His children, His body, *you and me,* to spread the gospel. If we stay on our butts all day and play video games and never do what God told us to do, many people will never know the Savior of the world. You *do not* need to be perfect to spread the gospel. You do not need to be some special Christian. Simply allow the Holy Spirit to use you.

DECLARATION:

Lord, send me. I will go. Jesus, You live inside of me. Greater is He who lives in me than he who is in the world. Jesus, You are greater. I am the light of the world. I am a born-again child of God. Jesus Christ, the greater one, lives inside of me.

God helps me to influence the world around me.
God, give me Your eyes.

Scripture Reading: Matthew 5

DAY 5

VIBING WITH POWER

But you will receive power when the Holy
Spirit comes on you... (Acts 1:8).

G od wants you to be a witness to the world of the amazing death and resurrection of Jesus Christ. Here is the thing: Anytime you have a witness, that witness must have *power*. Witnesses have to experience what they are talking about *firsthand*. Listen to what Jesus said to His first disciples:

> *It is not for you to know the times or dates the Father has set by his own authority. But you will receive power when the Holy Spirit comes on you; and you will be my witnesses in Jerusalem, and in all Judea and Samaria, and to the ends of the earth* (Acts 1:7–8).

Earlier in the chapter, in Acts 1:4–5, Jesus also said to them:

> *Do not leave Jerusalem, but wait for the gift my Father promised, which you have heard me speak about. For John baptized with water, but in a few days you will be baptized with the Holy Spirit.*

When we become born again, the Bible says that Jesus Christ now dwells within us, and so does the Holy Spirit. (The Holy Spirit is a person.) That being said, a deeper infilling of the Holy Spirit is promised to every Christian: the baptism of the Holy Spirit and fire. We see this in Matthew 3:11, where John the Baptist said,

> I baptize you with water for repentance. But after me comes one who is more powerful than I, whose sandals I am not worthy to carry. He [Jesus] will baptize you with the Holy Spirit and fire.

This scripture points to the difference between the baptism of water and the baptism of the Holy Spirit. Both baptisms are important for every believer, but they are not the same. The baptism in water symbolizes our spiritual death and resurrection in Christ. The baptism of the Holy Spirit is the anointing of the Spirit in a believer's life. It is important because Jesus wants you to be a *powerful witness* who is full of power so that you can change the world around you. Jesus wants you to run with Holy Spirit fire. Jesus said in Matthew 7:11,

> If you, then, though you are evil, know how to give good gifts to your children, how much more will your Father in heaven give good gifts to those who ask him!

The baptism of the Holy Spirit is for every child of God. Father God does not hold back good things from us, because He loves us. Choose to believe today that you can be on fire for God. Choose today to believe that you can be a powerful witness.

DECLARATION:

Father God, I thank You for Jesus. I thank You for the cross. Thank You for the blood. Thank You. I am saved. I am born again. I am forgiven. I am a brand-new creation in Christ Jesus. Lord, You are good, and Your mercy endures forever. I trust that You want the best for my life. I trust Your plan.

Scripture Reading: Acts 1

DAY 6

GO ALL THE WAY WITH GOD

Therefore I tell you, whatever you ask for in prayer, believe that you have received it, and it will be yours (Mark 11:24).

Have you ever gone to a pool with friends and discovered they only want to get their feet in? That is what you would call boring. Sadly, a lot of Christians are like this in their walk with God. They make an initial choice to follow after Jesus, but they don't really pursue anything more. When it comes to the baptism of the Holy Spirit, God wants you to be fully drenched in His amazing power. But you will not receive the baptism of the Holy Spirit accidentally.

No one goes to Golden Corral, eats five plates worth of food, and then expects to be in better physical shape. What you put in is what you will get out. The truth is, when it comes to your relationship with God, you have to *go in faith*. Do not think that God will just drop things accidentally into your life without you having any responsibility to do something with them. Think about how you got saved: *You* decided to believe the gospel and pray out loud to receive Jesus into your heart. God cannot make that choice for you. Everything else in your walk with God operates by *faith*.

When I was in middle school, if there was a girl I liked, instead of telling her directly and shooting my shot, I acted childishly and talked to her friends instead, having them pass on a message. Here is the thing: That is not how you get to know God. You cannot get closer to God just through other people. You must have a one-on-one relationship too. Take God at His word, and trust that He listens to you. Trust that the baptism of the Holy Spirit is for you. You do not need anyone else to be there with you for you to receive the gift. In fact, you can receive the baptism of the Holy Spirit right now.

Jesus said, in Mark 11:24, "Therefore I tell you, whatever you ask for in prayer, believe that you have received it, and it will be yours." Jesus did not say that you can believe for only 50 percent. He said, *"Whatever you ask in prayer!"* God does not work in accidental ways. If you want to be more on fire for Him, you must want what He has.

Today, I would like to lead you in a prayer to receive the baptism of the Holy Spirit. When you say *amen,* believe that Jesus has filled you with the Holy Spirit! It is a finished work. There are no exclusions or exceptions. Believe that Jesus will give you a prayer language that is not your native language. After you say *amen,* feel free to open your mouth and believe that tongues will flow out. It is important to know that the Holy Spirit will *help you* to pray in tongues. This means that, while the Holy Spirit will give you the ability, you have to walk it out yourself. It will be your tongue moving and your vocal chords working, but then the Holy Spirit will flow out from there.

DECLARATION:

Jesus, thank You for promising to send me the Holy Spirit. I trust Your word today. I ask You, right now, to baptize me in the Holy Spirit and fire. I believe I receive my prayer language. I believe from this point forward I am filled with the Holy Spirit and fire. I am on fire for You, Jesus. Thank You for the baptism of the Holy Spirit. In Jesus' name, amen.

Now open your mouth and pray. Praise God for His goodness. Allow your tongue to move, and trust that God will do it. Do not quit if you don't "feel" anything. Just keep going in faith.

Scripture Reading: Acts 2

DAY 7

DON'T LEAVE JESUS ON READ

The thief does not come except to steal, and to kill, and to destroy. I have come that they may have life, and that they may have it more abundantly (John 10:10 NKJV).

Let's imagine for a quick second that I slide into the messages of my crush and shoot my shot. To my surprise, it is going better than I expect, and she ends up saying *yes* to a date. (I am not saying you should do this; it's just an example of devotion.) So I tell her that I am going to pick her up at 7:00 PM at her house and take her to Chipotle. When I get to her house, I am feeling good, all ready for a date. But she never walks out. Instead, she sends a text two hours later saying, "I am so hungry; why didn't you get me food?" Now that girl is what they call *wildin'*. She is *not valid* for acting that way. After I have done everything I need to do—set the date, the time, and the place and then show up to meet her—this girl decides to go her own way. And then she blames me for her hunger.

Here's the thing: Millions of believers and non-believers all across the world have acted this way toward God. You see, God has hit us all up and given us His word (the Bible). God has given us Jesus Christ, who is our salvation. He has created a way out of sin and darkness and despair and hopelessness. God has set a date with every single person living on this earth. But so many of us choose to ghost Him. And then we blame Him for our problems. God is a good God. As Jesus said in John 10:10, "The thief does not come except to steal, and to kill, and to destroy. I have come that they may have life, and that they may have it more abundantly" (NKJV). Our problems aren't His fault.

Never forget that Jesus wants to be your best friend, so treat Him that way. He is never complicated. When He talks to you, don't leave Him on read (or heard). When He asks you to do something, do it. When something doesn't work out the way you wanted, instead of blaming Him, ask Him what you can change. Make your own decision that you will follow Him. What is amazing about Jesus is that you never have to doubt whether He has your back. He will always answer. He will always listen. He knows the best for your life.

But you must understand that the first and foremost way God will speak to you is through His word, the Bible. You must go where He is speaking. If I sent you a message on Instagram today, but you checked Facebook Messenger, who would be at fault? Could you blame me for not messaging you? *Heck no!* Many people blame God for not speaking, when He already has spoken through the Bible. Make a choice today that you will trust Him at His word. When you know that God has said something in His word, decide that you will do it.

DECLARATION:

God, I thank You for Your word. The Bible is God speaking to me. The Bible is God speaking to _____ [insert your name]. Lord, I am Your sheep, and I hear Your voice. I trust Your word. I

*will stand firm on Your word. I trust Your prom-
ises to me. God, I choose You today. I will follow
You all the days of my life. If I have fallen short or
allowed sin into my life, I repent. Forgive me of all
sin. I am Yours to command.*

Scripture Reading: James 1

DAY 8

HOW IT ALL STARTED

So God created mankind in his own image, in the image of God he created them; male and female he created them (Genesis 1:27).

Have you ever wondered how God actually created the world? I know you are thinking something like, "With His big hands, Gabe. Duh!" But actually, how did God create us? The Bible says *God spoke*, and then everything we know to be creation came into existence. We typically use our words to just communicate, but God has also shown us how to use words to *create*. Words are actually the most powerful force on earth. Now, before you ask your crush on a date, believing that your words will create feelings on his or her end, let me explain what this actually means. The Bible says:

> *In the beginning God created the heavens and the earth. Now the earth was formless and empty, darkness was over the surface of the deep, and the Spirit of God was hovering over the waters. And God said, "Let there be light," and there was light* (Genesis 1:1-3).

In Hebrew, that phrase in verse 4 can be more closely translated as "*Light be,* and *light was.*" The Bible also says, in Hebrews 11:3, "By faith we understand that the worlds have been framed by the word of God, so that what is seen hath not been made out of things which appear" (ASV).

Here is what is so amazing: We have been created in the image of God. In Genesis 1:27, it says, "God created mankind in his own image...." God expects us to use our words the way He uses words—to change the world around us. You can use your words to follow after God. When your words agree with God's word (the Bible), your life will line up with it. The Bible says, in James 3:4–5,

> Look also at ships: although they are so large and are driven by fierce winds, they are turned by a very small rudder wherever the pilot desires. Even so the tongue is a little member and boasts great things (NKJV).

So many people use their words to bring people down and complain. But by doing so, those people are actually bringing more problems onto themselves. They experience more problems, because it is actually a spiritual law: Your life is a reflection of the words you speak. Choose to speak words of life. Encourage others around you, including yourself. Speak the truth of God's word even when you don't feel it or see it happening. Do not allow your feelings to dominate. Instead, allow your faith to lead your thoughts and feelings.

DECLARATION:

God, thank You for today. Thank You for making me Your child. Thank You for creating me in Your image and likeness. Thank You for the words of life. Today, I make a decision that I will only speak the words of life. I am forgiven. I am washed in the blood of Jesus. I am powerful through Christ. I am called. I am chosen. I am loved in Your eyes. I choose to speak life and not death. I choose not to complain. Instead, I will give thanks and praise.

Scripture Reading: Genesis 1

DAY 9

"PRAY FOR ME TO NEVER FACE THE DEVIL"

We demolish arguments and every pretension that sets itself up against the knowledge of God, and we take captive every thought to make it obedient to Christ (2 Corinthians 10:5).

People always pull up in the social media comments like, "Gabe, pray for me. I just have these thoughts of doubt in my head. Pray that the thoughts would go away." Have you ever thought to yourself that you can control the birds that fly above your head? Probably not, because that would be crazy. But you do control whether or not you allow those birds to sit on your hair and make a nest. Thoughts are the same exact way. You will never be able to have perfect thoughts at all times. While we live here on this earth, we will face thoughts and feelings that are contrary to God's will. But that does *not* mean we should accept them. The Bible says, in 2 Corinthians 10:5,

> *We demolish arguments and every pretension that sets itself up against the knowledge of God, and we take captive every thought to make it obedient to Christ.*

Thoughts are like dating in high school: You cannot control who is in your class, but you can control who you date. What that means is that you always have to protect your heart from the enemy's thoughts. If you ever get a thought or idea that is evil or full of doubt, recognize that it's not from God *or you!* Do not get into guilt or shame just because you had the thought. Do not identify with a feeling of doubt and think that is who you are. Instead, reject that feeling or thought and choose to accept what God's word says.

The Bible says, in 1 Corinthians 2:16, "For, 'Who has known the mind of the Lord so as to instruct him?' But we have the mind of Christ." Believe today that you have the mind of Christ. The devil wants to convince you that you are a bad Christian because you had a negative thought or feeling come into your life. The truth is: The devil is actually the one who brings the thoughts, and then he blames it on you. Don't get played by him. Respond with the word of God and know that Jesus will always have your back.

DECLARATION:

Father, I thank You that I have the mind of Christ. I choose to believe Your word. I refuse thoughts and feelings of doubt. My mind is my mind. I take authority over every evil and impure thought and cast it out. My thoughts are lovely, just, pure, and a good report. I believe the best of people. I believe the best of situations. Father, help me to see people and situations the way You see them.

Scripture Reading: 2 Corinthians 10

DAY 10

A BUSSIN' SLURPEE

For it is by grace you have been saved, through faith—and this is not from yourselves, it is the gift of God (Ephesians 2:8).

The other day, I pulled up to a 7-Eleven store for a Slurpee. When I walked up to the cash register to pay, the employee told me just to take the Slurpee and leave. I asked him if he was for real, and he emphatically told me to leave the store before he changed his mind. I realized he was giving the Slurpee to me for free. All I had to do was receive it. When I got into my car, my only response was thankfulness. I was so thankful that God would use such a random event to bless me. But then I realized it wasn't an accident. God was showing me an example of His love to the world.

You see, Jesus has been given to the world as a *gift* from God. Sadly, just like I had a hard time receiving that free Slurpee, so many people doubt whether God really gave Jesus. It's so easy to think that things are too good to be true, because we have grown up with, "Excuse me, sir, I am calling to reach you about your car's extended warranty" and the phone pop-up notifications saying we won a free iPhone. The world is full of promises that are too good to be true. But Jesus is not one of them. He is amazing, *and* He really was sent from God for us.

The Bible says, "For it is by grace you have been saved, through faith—and this is not from yourselves, it is the gift of God" (Eph. 2:8). We do not need to be good enough to receive the righteousness of God. The Bible also says, "God made him who had no sin to be sin for us, so that in him we might become the righteousness of God" (2 Cor. 5:21). Jesus paid the full price of your sin and has given you His *exact* righteousness. God now sees us just like He sees Jesus. Choose today to believe this reality. Every day you may be tempted to think you are not good enough for the grace of God. The devil will remind you of your past mistakes and put feelings of shame and guilt on you. *Ain't nobody got time for that.* Refuse to accept those feelings and instead receive the love of God and truth of God's word.

DECLARATION:

Father, I thank You for the gift of Jesus. I thank You for Your unconditional love. Thank You for Your forgiveness. Thank You for Your grace. I choose to believe that You are for me. Greater is He who lives in me than he who is in the world. I am born again. I am a new creature. I am the righteousness of God in Christ Jesus. I am in right standing with God. I repent of all sin. I receive my cleansing. I am free in Jesus' name.

Scripture Reading: Ephesians 2

DAY 11

MOUNTAIN-MOVING FAITH

Now faith is confidence in what we hope for and assurance about what we do not see (Hebrews 11:1).

How many times do you wake up in the morning and *feel like going to school or work?* Now, unless you are one of those strange people who somehow loves to wake up early and sit in a building for eight hours and listen to the algorithmic theorem, your answer is probably something like *almost never.* That being said, hopefully in spite of your drowsiness and lack of motivation to wake up, you still get up and go to school or work, because you know it's what you must do. (Some of y'all are going to say you still don't get up, but for the sake of the example, just go with it.) My point here is that you would never question your status as a student or employee just because you don't feel like going to school or work.

This situation is similar to our relationship with God. So many of us struggle to be confident in our salvation and place in God's family because we don't *feel saved.* We don't *feel loved.* We don't *feel forgiven.* But the truth is that no matter how we feel, *God's word never changes.* A man named Smith Wigglesworth, who raised at least fourteen people from the dead, said, "I am not moved by what I feel. I am only moved by the Word of God." The Bible says, "Now faith is confidence in what we hope for and assurance about what we do not see" (Heb. 11:1). That means our faith is not based on our feelings, but on the word of God.

Have you ever walked into a restaurant and told the server that even though the menu says the steak is fifteen dollars, you only *feel like* paying five dollars? If you have, you know that play will not work. Most of us would never try it, because we know it's crazy dumb. So why do we then think our place in God changes *just because we don't feel saved?* One of the most important things we can learn about faith is that it is not based upon what we see or feel, but on the word of God. In the Bible, Jesus taught His disciples about faith:

> "Have faith in God," Jesus answered. "Truly I tell you, if anyone says to this mountain, 'Go, throw yourself into the sea,' and does not doubt in their heart but believes that what they say will happen, it will be done for them. Therefore I tell you, whatever you ask for in prayer, believe that you have received it, and it will be yours. And when you stand praying, if you hold anything against anyone, forgive them, so that your Father in heaven may forgive you your sins" (Mark 11:22–25).

If you want to have mountain-moving faith, this is the scripture God wants you to know.

DECLARATION:

I have mountain-moving faith. I choose to believe God's word. I am not moved by what I feel. I am not moved by what I see. I am only moved by what I believe. I trust God. I trust God's plan for my life. Father, thank You for putting breath in my lungs today. Show me Your word like never before. I forgive everyone who has wronged me. I choose to love others just like You love me. I choose to forgive others just like You forgave me.

Scripture Reading: Mark 11

DAY 12

MOUNTAIN-MOVING FAITH, PART 2

Therefore I tell you, whatever you ask for in prayer, believe that you have received it, and it will be yours (Mark 11:24).

I will never forget the morning when I shared about mountain-moving faith in my public high school in Virginia. About thirty kids had gathered in a side room of the library. My friends Sajjad and Cameron from my football team showed up. They were both deaf—Sajjad partially deaf and Cameron completely deaf in both ears. As I preached about faith that moves mountains, I sensed in my heart that something amazing was about to happen. At the end of the ten-minute message, we all stood up and prayed for a miracle. Sure enough, Sajjad and Cameron both received their hearing! We tested it afterward by having Cameron turn around and instructing him to raise his hand as soon as he heard us slam a chair into the table. Sure enough, his hand raised at the exact moment. Everyone was shaken, to say the least.

A lot of people think the faith Jesus talked about in Mark 11 was just for the original disciples. Others think miracles are just random. Most Christians think that whatever happens is up to God; who are we to say anything else? But the reality is that Jesus wants you to *choose to believe.* In Mark 11:24, He said, "Therefore I tell you, whatever you ask for in prayer, believe that you have received it, and it will be yours." Notice the emphasis Jesus placed on *you.* God cannot force you to believe. God cannot force you to love Him back. God cannot force you to do anything!

Here is the thing: Faith to move mountains is not just necessary for salvation. Faith is needed for every single day. It is needed for school and friends and family and literally every single thing you will face in life. When Jesus said your faith in God will move mountains, those mountains represent any and every problem we have here on earth. Jesus has given us the key to victory: Faith in His word. When you have faith in God, you will not wait for the problem to change before you believe that God is working. Instead, you will believe He is at work *as soon as you say amen.* Once you pray, you believe you have the answer, and you move forward.

Let's say you are praying for a loved one to be saved. Jesus said, "Ask the Lord of the harvest, therefore, to send out workers into his harvest field" (Matt. 9:38). When you pray for God to help your family and send the gospel into their lives, as soon as you ask Him to do it and say *amen,* believe that it is finished! Believe that God has already started to send the right people at the right time into your family. You can apply this principle in any area of your life. Once you have the scripture, stand on that word and believe that once you say *amen,* God is already busy at work answering your prayer.

DECLARATION:

Father, I pray right now for my family and friends. I ask You to send laborers across their paths so that they can know You. Open up their eyes. Reveal the light of Your gospel. Use me to spread Your love everywhere I go. Thank You for making me a vessel of Your love. I am a vessel of light.

Scripture Reading: Matthew 17

LIVING WORRY-FREE

Casting all your care upon Him, for He cares for you (1 Peter 5:7 NKJV).

Have you ever been blessed with the chance to take a test with a partner? That is the best kind of test possible. It's always hilarious to see everyone chase down the smart kids they never wanted to talk to before. When I took AP Chemistry, I really did not have a clue what I was doing. *But* I made sure to always surround myself with people who did. And when the time came for me to complete those group tests, I always relied on my smart friends to get the job done. I did not deserve to have them as my partners for the test. Many times, I didn't study as much as they did, and I didn't know nearly as much as they did. But I was blessed by their help and partnership on those tests.

It is a lot like how God has given us a partner in life who is *built different*: Jesus Christ. We don't just have to rely on Him for a few things. We have been called to rely on and trust in Him for 100 percent of our lives. The Bible describes that as "Casting all your care upon Him, for He cares for you" (1 Pet. 5:7 NKJV). God knows the best plan for our lives. God knows how to take care of every problem we will ever face. The good news is, even when we don't feel qualified or good enough, His grace will always be there for us.

When we worry and feel anxious about any part of our lives, we are trying to take care of our problems on our own—*which will never work*. God wants to take 100 percent of the worry and care. When we choose to cast our cares on God, He will then work for us. If we try to be good enough on our own and worry our way through life, God is left on the sideline. We will regret that outcome every time. No one else can care for you like Jesus. No one else can work for you like Jesus. When we humble ourselves and recognize that God is greater, we give Him a place to perform miracles.

Worrying will never change anything. It will only make our lives worse. But when we place our faith in God's will and ability, we will see the situation turn around. When I played football in high school, countless times I would start to get nervous and worry when I saw the size of the opposing team. But my worry never helped me become stronger or faster. When I chose to trust God for the game instead, He always had my back.

DECLARATION:

God, I choose today to cast all my cares on You. I refuse to worry. I refuse to fear. I refuse to have anxiety. Lord, I throw all of my worries and cares on You. I trust You, Jesus. I trust that Your plan is best. I cast the care of _____ [insert your specific worry] over on You. In Jesus' name, I will never take that care and worry back. That care is now Yours, Lord. I trust You, and I will do what You tell me to do.

Scripture Reading: 1 Peter 5

BUILT DIFFERENT

DAY 14

LIVING FEAR-FREE

Let not your heart be troubled; you believe in
God, believe also in Me (John 14:1 NKJV).

When I was in eighth grade, I was a scrawny boy, but I played JV football. Our first game was against a team from two hours south. When we first showed up, we felt pretty confident—until we heard a thunderous sound from the stairs above. In shock, I watched the large human beings on the opposing team enter the field. All of our previous confidence vanished. The opposing team looked several years older than us. I have no clue what they were feeding those boys, but they were definitely built differently. We caught the loss that night for sure. I also think I got concussed, but I can't remember for sure. On that night, we did not have a good reason to be confident. But, if by some miracle, our varsity team had pulled up in a bus and backed us up, we certainly would have caught the dub (the victory). If we had seen our varsity team joining us to play, our confidence would have returned.

Jesus said, "Let not your heart be troubled, you believe in God, believe also in Me" (John 14:1 NKJV). If we can gain confidence from the knowledge that our friends and family have our backs, how much more can we be confident in life knowing that Jesus is fully behind us? Every day, we have a choice: to fear or to *fear not*. The majority of Christians think they can't do anything to change the level of fear in their lives. But Jesus literally told us to *fear not*. The devil tries to convince us to be afraid because we cannot handle life on our own. But that is the thing: *we are not alone*. The Bible says, "Do not be afraid or terrified because of them, for the Lord your God goes with you; he will never leave you nor forsake you" (Deut. 31:6).

Fear is just contaminated faith. Fear is having faith in the devil. Fear is having faith that whatever you are worried about will end up coming to pass. Turn fear on its head and choose to have faith *in God*. Have faith that God is working and moving. Have faith that the word of God will come to pass. Have you ever rinsed out a half-full glass of milk? When you first start filling it with water, it gets a little murky. But as time passes and more water flows through the glass, the milk is automatically displaced. That is exactly what happens when you choose to fill yourself up with the word of God. Any fear or stress or worry will start to be displaced by the power of God's word.

DECLARATION:

Father God, I thank You for Your word. Today, I refuse to fear. I choose to fill myself up with faith. Father, fill me up today with Your overflowing love. Spirit of fear, I rebuke you. Leave my family. Leave my friends. Perfect love casts out all fear. I have been perfected in love.

Scripture Reading: John 14

LET'S TALK ABOUT LOVE

For God so loved the world that he gave his one and only Son, that whoever believes in him shall not perish but have eternal life (John 3:16).

When you read that title, you may have thought about that crush you are romantically interested in. But today we are learning about a different love. It's called the God kind of love—*agape*. The God kind of love is always so much more than conditional human love. The New Testament uses the Greek word for God's love, *agape,* more than two hundred times. John 15:13 says, "Greater love [*agape*] has no one than this: to lay down one's life for one's friends." The Bible also says:

> *For God so loved* [agape] *the world that he gave his one and only Son, that whoever believes in him shall not perish but have eternal life. For God did not send his Son into the world to condemn the world, but to save the world through him* (John 3:16–17).

Jesus did not die for perfect people. The blood of Jesus was not shed because we are something good. God's love was not even a logical investment. It was reckless. Why would God send His Son to die for sinners who rejected

Him? The answer is simple: because His love is *not* conditional. God will never stop loving you. God will never stop being there for you. He will never stop chasing you down. The song "Reckless Love" by Cory Asbury is an awesome expression of this truth. In order to have strong faith, you must understand God's love for you. You must understand that no sin or mistake can ever separate you from Him. He does not love you because of who you are—but because of *who He is*. If Jesus died to save sinners—those who deserve nothing—what makes you think He will stop loving you when you make a mistake? What makes you think your failure is stronger than His blood? *Nothing* is stronger than the blood of Jesus.

Imagine that Jeff Bezos randomly gave you a million dollars with no strings attached. But the next day, you only get a C on your physics test. Do you think Jeff Bezos would take that gift back? If the gift was given with no strings attached, he would *never* demand you do something to earn it. In life, we are so used to earning things, but God's love can never be earned or lost. That is why the Bible says,

> *Beloved, let us love one another, for love is from God, and whoever loves has been born of God and knows God. Anyone who does not love does not know God, because God is love* (1 John 4:7–8 ESV).

God will never stop loving you, because He is love, and He will never stop existing.

DECLARATION:

Father God, I believe You love me. I thank You for sending Jesus Christ to die on the cross for me. Your agape love is unconditional. Jesus, I love You back. I choose to return what You gave. Open up my eyes so that I can understand how You see me. Open up my eyes so that I can see like You see. God, You love me just as much as You love Jesus. I am accepted in Your sight. I am accepted in Your love.

Scripture Reading: 1 John 4

CATCH A DUB EVERY DAY

But thanks be to God! He gives us victory through
our Lord Jesus Christ (1 Corinthians 15:57).

I don't know about you, but I *hate losing*. I played almost every sport growing up, and I always did my best to win. That desire to succeed, which every human has, is actually God-given. To catch L's in life is basically to be copying the devil, because let's be honest, this guy caught the ultimate L when Jesus rose again from the dead. The Bible says, "But thanks be to God! He gives us victory through our Lord Jesus Christ" (1 Cor. 15:57). Christians are not called to be lowly worms in the dirt. It is time that we have a winner's mentality. Winners do not get caught up or slowed down by their mistakes. Instead, they keep moving forward with their head up, knowing they will always have the advantage. Even when it doesn't look like it or feel like it, a winner will always believe in the desired outcome.

The Bible describes God as the one "who gives life to the dead and calls those things which do not exist as though they did" (Rom. 4:17 NKJV). As children of God, we have been made in His image. Just as God calls those things that are not as though they are, we are now called to speak faith-filled words that often go against what we see and feel. When you feel hopeless, that is the best time to speak words of hope. You will never grow and get stronger if you just allow yourself to stay in the struggle. You must decide that you are not going to stay where you are.

Recently, I flew from Pittsburgh to Dallas, and I needed to take my electric skateboard with me. I knew that when I went through security, it might get flagged, and there was a chance the airline wouldn't let me take it. Sure enough, security took the board to the side and started questioning me. I remember feeling so nervous, I was about to pee myself. But I knew that if I was confident in my understanding of the skateboard and my right to carry it with me, I might have a chance. So I walked up to the security officer, made direct eye contact, and assured him that the board was safe for flying and that I would take it with me. Most people might say I was tripping, but the TSA officer looked at the board a couple more times and then reluctantly let me have it. I learned that day that confidence is everything in this life. If we can be confident about a skateboard that maybe should not go on planes, how much more confident can we choose to be in the God who created the heavens and the earth, the Alpha and Omega, the everlasting one?

DECLARATION:

Father God, I am confident in Your word. I am confident in my salvation. I am confident of my healing through the blood of Jesus. I am confident that I am forgiven. I am confident that my past is gone. I am a brand-new creation in Christ Jesus. I am a winner and not a loser. I have a winner's mentality. God, together we catch victory every day. Show me areas of my life that I can change and improve to look more like You, Jesus.

Scripture Reading: 1 Corinthians 15

DAY 17

LIVING A THANKFUL LIFE

*Enter his gates with thanksgiving and his courts with praise;
give thanks to him and praise his name* (Psalm 100:4).

Every human being on this planet has a deep desire to know our creator. One of the most important lessons we can learn about our relationship with God is *how to be thankful*. The Bible says:

> *Enter his gates with thanksgiving and his courts with praise; give thanks to him and praise his name. For the Lord is good and his love endures forever; his faithfulness continues through all generations* (Psalm 100:4–5).

When we come to God in prayer, instead of just bringing Him our struggles and complaints, we are called to give Him thanks. It is easy to look at your life and find all the wrong things going on, but God wants you to recognize the *good* and praise Him for it. Maybe your mom doesn't get you all the food you want, but hopefully you do have *some* food in the fridge. I remember always thinking the fridge was empty—until I moved out and had to get food on my own. At that point, I realized the fridge in my parents' house was a lot fuller than I thought. Don't wait to be thankful till you get to heaven; be thankful now. When we choose to live grateful lives, we will experience the joy and hope God called us to have.

Have you ever met a huge complainer who has a lot of friends? That almost never happens, because no one wants to hang out with someone who complains. I am not saying God will ghost you if you are not thankful, but God cannot be real *to you* if you don't want Him to be. When we have thankful spirits, we will experience God on another level. When you pray today, look at your life and be quick to find the positives. Give thanks for your family members, friends, freedoms, country, and life that you have. Be as specific as you can. When you give thanks to God, His presence fills the room. God loves to be in places where He is honored and recognized. Get excited about everything He is doing in your life. The grass is *always* greener when you have God on your side.

DECLARATION:

Father, thank You for today. Thank You for the breath inside my lungs. Thank You for my family. Thank You for my friends. Thank You for saving me. I am forgiven. I am born again. I am baptized in the Holy Spirit. My past is gone. You have such a good plan for my life. God, thank You for caring for me. Jesus, thank You for giving everything for me. Jesus, You paid the price. Thank You for setting me free.

Scripture Reading: Psalm 100

HOW TO HEAR GOD'S VOICE

He calls his own sheep by name and leads them out (John 10:3).

We have all probably taken a test in which we found ourselves wishing the teacher would say the answer to just *that one question*. If we so desperately desire to hear the teacher give us the answers, how much more should we want to hear from the creator of the universe so that He can guide us through every day? The truth is: God knows the perfect plan for our lives and wants to help us walk in it. If you are able to hear God's voice and put His plan into action, you *will accomplish* everything He has told you to do. Jesus said:

> *The gatekeeper opens the gate for him, and the sheep listen to his voice. He calls his own sheep by name and leads them out. When he has brought out all his own, he goes on ahead of them, and his sheep follow him because they know his voice. But they will never follow a stranger; in fact, they will run away from him because they do not recognize a stranger's voice* (John 10:3–5).

Imagine for a minute that I sent you a DM on Instagram, but you only ever open your iMessages. Because you never saw my DM, you may think I forgot about you, but you were simply looking in the wrong place. When God speaks to us, He speaks to our *spirits*. The Bible says, "The human spirit is the lamp of the Lord that sheds light on one's inmost being" (Prov. 20:27). This means that when God speaks to us, He speaks to our *hearts*. I hear so many young Christians say, "I feel like God isn't speaking," or, "I just can't hear His voice." Even though you may feel the same way, it is time to believe what Jesus said. He said we are His sheep, and we hear His voice. *That is the truth.*

God is always speaking, and we always have the chance to hear His voice. The key is that we *tune in*. If a banger song is playing on the radio in FM, but we only turn on AM, we will never hear it. We cannot expect to hear God's voice when we are only tuned into fleshly desires here on earth. When we fill ourselves with Netflix shows, TikToks, and video games—when those things take up our time instead of the word of God—it will become more and more difficult to hear His voice clearly. But when we choose to open our Bibles and worship God and spend time with Him, it will become much easier. Also, even when we don't feel it or see it, we must choose to speak words of faith, believing that *we are God's sheep, and we do indeed hear His voice.*

DECLARATION:

Father, I thank You that I am Your sheep, and I hear Your voice. Jesus, I will follow You today. Lead me in the paths of righteousness for Your name's sake. I do not follow the voice of the stranger. I do not follow the voice of my flesh. I do not follow other people's opinions. God, I will follow Your voice. I am a child of God. I know my Father's voice. Thank You for speaking to me today.

Now take some time to get quiet and listen to God today as He speaks. Be sure to tune out the distractions.

Scripture Reading: John 10

DAY 19

THE FAMILY OF GOD

For this reason I kneel before the Father, from whom
every family in heaven and on earth derives its name

(Ephesians 3:14–15).

When I was eighteen, I moved out of my parents' house to attend Bible school. I packed my bags and traveled more than one thousand miles from Virginia to Texas to fulfill God's plan for my life. As you can imagine, my parents were not too thrilled about me leaving them to move to Fort Worth. But when December came rolling around, I never questioned whether or not they would let me back for Christmas. In fact, as soon as I got off the flight, they were there to pick me up. Even though I had been gone for months, my family status stayed the same. When I came home, I never questioned whether I could run to the fridge and eat whatever I wanted.

God the Father wants you to know today that no matter how far you have traveled from His house, you are always welcomed back. The Bible says, "For this reason I kneel before the Father, from whom every family in heaven and on earth derives its name" (Eph. 3:14–15). While you may be known here on earth by your birth father's name, your true identity is now found in Christ Jesus. God the Father is now *your Father*. (Cue the Star Wars line, "Luke, I am your father....") When you see yourself in the mirror, see yourself as a child of the Most High God. Keep your head up high.

Revelation 1:6 says that Jesus has "made us to be a kingdom and priests to serve his God and Father—to him be glory and power for ever and ever! Amen." It is not prideful to call yourself royalty. In Him that is what you are. Just know that the King of kings and the Lord of lords is the one who deserves all the glory. It is actually humility to accept what God says about you and let the world know the truth. Because our Father God is built different, we are built different. Because we are children of God, we now have *His DNA.*

We all know kids who look almost exactly like their father or mother in the natural. In the spirit, we have a responsibility to look more and more like Jesus every day. We can do that by looking into His word. Have you ever gone to school or work without looking in the mirror? That is what you call an L. Your hair will be messy and you'll probably have three boogers too. But if you look in the mirror, you will be able to straighten things out and have an awesome day. We must look into the mirror of the word of God so that we can realize the areas of our lives that we can change to look more like Jesus.

DECLARATION:

I am a child of God. God is my Father. I am born again. I am a new creation in Christ Jesus. I have the DNA of Father God. God, show me what I need to change today. I want to look more like Jesus today. Give me Your eyes. Give me Your

*ears. Give me Your heart. Here I am, Lord; send
me. I will go.*

Scripture Reading: Revelation 1

DAY 20

MEDITATING GOD'S WAY

Be strong and very courageous. Be careful to
obey all the law my servant Moses gave you; do
not turn from it to the right or to the left, that you
may be successful wherever you go (Joshua 1:7).

W hen we hear the word *meditation,* many people think of Buddhist monks sitting in the lotus position. But meditation is actually a concept that comes from God. The devil does not create anything. He just takes things from God and perverts them. In the Bible, God told Joshua:

> *Be strong and very courageous. Be careful to obey all the law my servant Moses gave you; do not turn from it to the right or to the left, that you may be successful wherever you go. Keep this Book of the Law always on your lips; meditate on it day and night, so that you may be careful to do everything written in it. Then you will be prosperous and successful. Have I not commanded you? Be strong and courageous. Do not be afraid; do not be discouraged, for the Lord your God will be with you wherever you go* (Joshua 1:7–9).

This word that God gave to Joshua is an example for all believers. We fill ourselves up by meditating on God's word. When we read the Bible, sometimes it helps to quickly pour through the chapters, but sometimes we need to focus on just *one verse or passage*. To meditate, take one scripture verse or passage and become solely focused on it. Speak it out loud multiple times and close your eyes. Imagine and picture that scripture in your head. As you meditate and continue speaking the scripture out loud, you will find yourself strengthened.

I don't know about you, but my short attention span makes me feel like my brain is always going in one thousand different directions. God knows we can be so distracted sometimes, and that is why He gave us meditation. It is important to find the scripture you need for whatever problem you are currently facing, and meditate *on that scripture*. This is as easy as Google searching scriptures on a particular topic. Once you have the scripture, set it as your wallpaper. Speak it as many times as you can. Close your eyes and quiet your mind. Just as your mind can be consumed with thinking about sports, your crush, or a TV show, your mind can also be consumed by the word of God. We were created to be addicted to the word of God.

DECLARATION:

Lord, today I choose to meditate on Your word. Your words are life to me. I am strong and courageous. I refuse to fear. I will not turn to the left or the right. I will stay right on course. I will fulfill God's plan for my life. I will fulfill my destiny. I will do everything God wants me to do. God, I put

Your word first. Lord, thank You for always being with me. You have my side. You have my back.

Scripture Reading: Joshua 1

DAY 21

GOD'S GRACE

What shall we say, then? Shall we go on sinning
so that grace may increase? (Romans 6:1).

Have you ever wondered, *If I keep sinning, will God still forgive me?* Maybe you question whether God will still forgive you if you commit *a specific sin* or have a certain addiction. The Bible says:

> *What shall we say, then? Shall we go on sinning*
> *so that grace may increase? By no means! We*
> *are those who have died to sin; how can we live*
> *in it any longer? Or don't you know that all of us*
> *who were baptized into Christ Jesus were bap-*
> *tized into his death? We were therefore buried*
> *with him through baptism into death in order*
> *that, just as Christ was raised from the dead*
> *through the glory of the Father, we too may live*
> *a new life* (Romans 6:1–4).

The Bible also promises, "If we confess our sins, he is faithful and just and will forgive us our sins and purify us from all unrighteousness" (1 John 1:9). When we look at these two scriptures, we can see that: 1) Yes, God does forgive us of *all sin,* but also, 2) This grace that God gives does *not* mean we can go out and sin more. Jesus did not die on the cross so that we can freely sin. Jesus died on the cross so that we could be *free from sin*. God's grace is the power that has freed us from the bondage of our sin.

We must view ourselves the way God views us. We do not have God's grace because we earned it. We have God's grace because He freely gave it to us. That means we cannot lose it if we make a mistake. It would be like if a random stranger bought ice cream for you at Dairy Queen, but because you didn't have money in your wallet, as you were leaving you gave the ice cream back. You didn't feel good enough to keep it. That might be the stupidest thing I have ever heard. The sad truth is: That is how sad God feels when we think we lost our salvation because we made a mistake.

When we begin to fully understand God's love for us, His love will motivate us to *sin less*. God's love will motivate us to *crucify the flesh*. To crucify the flesh *does not* mean nailing your hand to a cross. It means choosing to feed your spirit instead of feeding earthly desires like gluttony, drunkenness, fornication, time-wasting, and so forth. Instead of focusing on sin and whether a certain action is sin, ask yourself how that action will affect your relationship with God. When you understand how much God loves you, you will not want to hurt Him.

DECLARATION:

Lord, thank You for Your grace. Thank You for loving me. Thank You for saving me. The blood of Jesus has cleansed me of all sin. I am free from sin. I am free from addictions. I am free from chains. I am free. Whom the Son sets free is free indeed. I am no longer a slave to fear. I am a child of God. I am called. I am redeemed.

Scripture Reading: Romans 6

BUILT DIFFERENT

DAY 22

KNOW YOUR COVENANT WITH GOD

The Lord who rescued me from the paw of the lion and the paw of the bear will rescue me from the hand of this Philistine (1 Samuel 17:37).

Imagine that your teacher tells you the next day's test will be open note, but then when the next day comes, she tells you that she changed her mind and the test won't be open note. If you are anything like me, you would be feeling salty. She said something (her covenant), but then she broke it. Maybe you have had a friend tell you that your secrets were safe with him or her—but then you heard those same secrets being spread abroad at school. *Covenant* is just a big word for "agreement"; it can also mean "contract" or "promise." While human beings sometimes have a hard time keeping their word, God *always* keeps His word. God is the perfect example of a covenant keeper. God is the most faithful friend you could possibly have.

Everyone knows the story about David and Goliath, but most people don't understand *how exactly* David took down Goliath. David's victory had more to do with his understanding of God's word than it did with luck or God's will. On that day, God willed that Israel would defeat the Philistines, but it was not happening. Instead, everyone on Israel's side was afraid and forgot that they had God on their side. Everyone except David. He knew he was part of God's team. We see this in 1 Samuel 17:

> But David said to Saul, "Your servant has been keeping his father's sheep. When a lion or a bear came and carried off a sheep from the flock, I went after it, struck it and rescued the sheep from its mouth. When it turned on me, I seized it by its hair, struck it and killed it. Your servant has killed both the lion and the bear; this uncircumcised Philistine will be like one of them, because he has defied the armies of the living God. The Lord who rescued me from the paw of the lion and the paw of the bear will rescue me from the hand of this Philistine" (1 Samuel 17:34–37).

It is no coincidence that the only man with confidence in God that day also ended up being the only man to catch the victory. Look at what happened next:

> David said to the Philistine, "You come against me with sword and spear and javelin, but I come against you in the name of the Lord Almighty, the God of the armies of Israel, whom you have defied. This day the Lord will deliver you into my hands, and I'll strike you down and cut off your head. This very day I will give the carcasses of the Philistine army to the birds and the wild animals, and the whole world will know that there is a God in Israel. All those gathered here will know that it is not by sword or spear that the Lord

saves; for the battle is the Lord's, and he will give all of you into our hands."

As the Philistine moved closer to attack him, David ran quickly toward the battle line to meet him. Reaching into his bag and taking out a stone, he slung it and struck the Philistine on the forehead. The stone sank into his forehead, and he fell facedown on the ground (1 Samuel 17:45–49).

David saw God move miraculously in his life that day *because he trusted that God would keep His covenant with His people Israel.* Just as God kept His old covenant with Israel, He now keeps His new covenant with us, because we have been grafted into His family.

DECLARATION:

God, thank You for Your covenant. Thank You for being faithful. I call You faithful, Lord. I trust that You have my back. Jesus, thank You for signing that covenant in Your blood. I will stand on Your word.

Scripture Reading: 1 Samuel 17

TAKE THE EXTRA WEIGHT OFF

Therefore, since we are surrounded by such a great cloud of witnesses, let us throw off everything that hinders and the sin that so easily entangles (Hebrews 12:1).

The devil wants to weigh our hearts down with distractions and sin and dead weight—things that are not important or crucial to the plan of God for us. Dead weight can include things like watching too much secular content on YouTube, TikTok, or Netflix, or playing too many video games. It could also be strife with your family and friends. Many times in my life, I knew God was working mightily in me, but then I would make a mistake and get sidetracked by a distraction. The Bible says:

> *Therefore, since we are surrounded by such a great cloud of witnesses, let us throw off everything that hinders and the sin that so easily entangles. And let us run with perseverance the race marked out for us, fixing our eyes on Jesus, the pioneer and perfecter of faith. For the joy set before him he endured the cross, scorning its shame, and sat down at the right hand of the throne of God. Consider him who endured such*

opposition from sinners, so that you will not grow weary and lose heart (Hebrews 12:1–3).

Here, God clearly tells us to throw off the distractions and instead run an all-out race toward God and His purposes for us. God wants us to be strong in spirit, not chunky in the flesh. Following after the flesh—allowing the distractions and dead weights—will only cause us to gain excess spiritual chunk that slows us down. It's time we cut out the parts of our lives that weigh us down. We need to be spiritually fit to be in the army of the Lord.

If you have pride about your life and think you have everything figured out and you don't need any change—you are in the wrong. We must have a spirit of humility to become what God wants us to be. To shed the excess weight, we need to be humble enough to admit we need a better workout and a healthier diet. When we do, God will be our trainer and get us spiritually fit for His army.

DECLARATION:

God, thank You for today. I do not want to be weighed down in life. Reveal to me any sin or weight that is slowing me down. I want to run for You, Jesus. I will run my race and finish my course. I see You today, Jesus. I set my eyes above and not below. I have a heavenly mindset.

Scripture Reading: Hebrews 12

DAY 24

KEEPING YOUR JOY

...For the joy of the Lord is your strength (Nehemiah 8:10).

One of the most powerful witnesses of our salvation in Jesus Christ is the joy that we possess. Should the locker room of a team that just won be silent in depression? No. And as Christians, after receiving the victory Jesus Christ won for us on the cross, we should not allow ourselves to wallow in sadness and depression. *Ain't nobody got time for that.* Instead, in the Bible, Nehemiah told the people of Israel,

> *Go and enjoy choice food and sweet drinks, and send some to those who have nothing prepared. This day is holy to our Lord. Do not grieve, for the joy of the Lord is your strength* (Nehemiah 8:10).

Many people think joy is an outcome of their circumstances. When things are going well, you will have joy. When things aren't going well, no joy. But God wants you to know that *you already have the joy of the Lord.* And you have a choice about whether you will walk in that joy.

During my sophomore year in high school, as I was walking down the hallway, I felt a tap on my shoulder. When I turned around, I was shocked to see a kid I used to bully in middle school. (Let's just say Gabe did not live a committed life for God back then.) He asked me a simple question: *"What happened to you?"* He said he saw such a difference in my life since middle school, that I carried a joy that he hadn't seen before. In response, I told him about how Jesus had changed my life, and I invited him to a Bible study. I realized that day that the most powerful witness for Jesus often is not in our words, but in our actions and our smile.

Jesus did not die on the cross with nails in His hands and a spear in His side so that we could live a depressed life. Jesus was crucified and rose again so that we could experience *His* joy—the kind of joy He possessed. Every day, we have a choice: What will we focus on? Will we choose to focus on all the issues and problems, or will we instead place our eyes on Jesus and the salvation He has freely given us? Will we choose to focus on our (possibly) annoying siblings, or will we focus on the unconditional love that God has provided us? I don't know about you, but I am going to focus on my mansion in heaven. I am going to focus on those eternal rewards. I am going to focus on the love of our Father. Join me. Let's have the joy of the Lord *every day*. Rejoice, and again I say *rejoice*!

DECLARATION:

I have the joy of the Lord. Father, I choose to focus on Your word today. I focus on the salvation You have given me. I choose to focus on my mansion in heaven. Thank You for loving me unconditionally. I refuse to accept depression. I am not sad. I am full of light. I am full of life. I am full of love. I am full of joy. Nothing is going to steal my joy.

The joy of the Lord is my strength! [Say that three times!]

Scripture Reading: Nehemiah 8

THE LORD IS OUR SHEPHERD

The Lord is my shepherd... (Psalm 23:1).

J esus is a great leader. He is not pushy, touchy, or controlling. I remember feeling like I could never please my football coach in high school because he always had such a tough face. Maybe you have had a teacher or coach who was like that in your life. God is different. The Bible says:

> *The Lord is my shepherd, I lack nothing. He makes me lie down in green pastures, he leads me beside quiet waters, he refreshes my soul. He guides me along the right paths for his name's sake* (Psalm 23:1–3).

You never have to worry or fear when Jesus is your shepherd. When you feel confused and darkness is surrounding your life, don't forget that Jesus has your back. When sheep are following their shepherd, they don't have to think about how their next step will logically affect the end result. They just trust their shepherd and follow his steps.

Some people on Instagram always try to be extra, making all these poses and faces they would never make in real life. Then they try to figure out how to get more likes and comments for their clout. The good news is, you don't have to be extra to follow Jesus. In fact, it's a lot better to keep it simple. Don't try to figure out everything on your own. God knows your life, and He knows His plan for you. Faith does not need to know all the answers. Instead, faith will simply walk step by step. No one can hike a mountain in just one wild leap. You would be some crazy alien if you could. In order to get up a mountain, you have to take it step by step. A NFL football player does not become jacked by lifting weights just one time. Don't get disappointed if your faith isn't where you want it to be. Instead, just make a choice to take a step up today. Even if the end looks far away, it is still within reach. When I graduated from high school, I thought to myself how quickly the four years went by. But during my sophomore year, I thought high school would never end. The times of great struggle, when you feel despair, are the exact times when you have to decide that you will not quit, that you will keep moving forward. Your faith will be proven when it's tested. Take joy in the test, because God will see you through.

DECLARATION:

Lord, thank You for being my shepherd. I shall not want. You lead me in the paths of righteousness. I will fear no evil. I will fulfill my destiny. I will do everything You have asked me to do. Lord, I trust You. I refuse to worry. Thank You for leading me beside still waters. Soul, be at peace, be still. Jesus, I will follow You today.

Scripture Reading: Psalm 23

DAY 26

HAVING A HEAVENLY MINDSET

If then you were raised with Christ, seek those
things which are above, where Christ is, sitting
at the right hand of God (Colossians 3:1 NKJV).

When I was in first grade, I had no greater fear than having my daily card moved down a step because Mrs. Troxell thought I was out of line. I felt exposed in front of everyone when I had to get up in front of the whole class and move my card down a level. When I look back on first grade, I realize that I was worried about a lot of things that didn't truly matter. Yes, it might have sucked moving that card down, but it never impacted anything; it was just a card. Way more important things exist in life. It may have seemed like everything back then, but now no one cares whether I was class pet or not. If you are reading this book, you probably aren't in first grade any-more, and you can relate to what I'm saying. The truth is, no matter how old we are, we can get caught up in temporary things instead of focusing on what is eternal. The Bible says, in Colossians 3:1–3,

> *If then you are raised with Christ, seek those*
> *things which are above, where Christ is, sitting at*
> *the right hand of God. Set your mind on things*

above, not on things on the earth. For you died, and your life is hidden with Christ in God (NKJV).

One day in heaven, we will look back at our lives on earth and realize that we got caught up in so many unnecessary burdens that we thought were important. Eternity is the most weighty and crucial part of the lives we live here on earth. Everything we do for the gospel's sake will always stick with us. If I gave you a million dollars today, but you only had it for ten seconds, would it be worth anything? In the grand scheme of time, one hundred years on earth may feel long, but one hundred years compared to millions and billions of years is nothing. Make a choice today to make the most of your time, to focus on your heavenly calling, to spread this gospel, to love one another. We are still breathing because God still has a plan for us every day.

DECLARATION:

Father, thank You for the time You have given me today. Help me to focus on what is right. Help me to focus on heavenly things and not on this earth. Lord, show me what is important to You. What's important to You is important to me. What doesn't matter as much to You doesn't matter as much to me. Jesus, I love You.

Scripture Reading: Colossians 3

DAY 27

EAT DIFFERENT TO BE DIFFERENT

...Man shall not live by bread alone, but by every word of God (Luke 4:4 NKJV).

My roommate Nik always jokes with me that I can't say I want a jawline but then eat twinkies and apple pies all day. As much as it hurts me to admit it, he is absolutely right. You can't expect to eat junk food and then become healthy. Yet somehow, so many of us, as Christians, think we can have strong faith by only going to church occasionally and reading the Bible once or twice a week. The truth is, we have to love God and His word more than anything else in this life.

When tempted by the devil, Jesus said, "...Man shall not live by bread alone, but by every word of God" (Luke 4:4 NKJV). Just as we should eat three meals a day to feed our bodies, we also have to eat up the word of God throughout our day if we want to be built different spiritually. When I say *spiritually*, I am not talking about some paranormal activity. Instead, *spiritually* refers to your heart, your inner person, the part of you that connects with God. This is the part of us that is fed by reading the word of God. About God's word, the psalmist said, "How sweet are your words to my taste, sweeter than honey to my mouth" (Ps. 119:103). When we read the Bible, we are eating up God's thoughts. If I send you a text on Instagram, that text becomes a container for my thoughts. That is what the Bible is in relation to God—and it is so much more.

When we take in God's word and read it out loud to ourselves, faith rises in us, and it will be like eating a good spiritual steak dinner. Babies don't eat meat, because all they can handle is milk. The same applies to our spiritual diet. We start out with milk, with the basics of the gospel, which is important. But at some point, we need to grow up and start eating the meat of the word. Here is what's amazing: How much you grow is dependent on how hungry you are for Him. You will not grow spiritually just because time passes, you attend church, or you open the Bible. Spiritual growth happens when you consume the word of God and then put it into action (exercise). Make a decision today that you will increase your spiritual intake of the word and then do what the Bible says.

DECLARATION:

Lord, Your words are life to me. I will not live by bread alone, but by every word from You. Help me to understand Your words today. I am thirsty for You. I am hungry for You. I am desperate to know You more every day. Set me on fire today so that I can burn for You. When You speak to me, I will listen. When I have Your word, I will put it into action.

Scripture Reading: Luke 4

DAY 28

THE ANOINTING

*The Spirit of the Lord is on me, because he has anointed
me to proclaim good news to the poor...* (Luke 4:18).

Some people, when they hear the word *anointing,*
might think of oil, but *anointing* actually represents a
special ability or grace. You can kind of compare it to
a boost-up in a video game. That boost-up gives you something special that you didn't have before. Jesus, after He was
baptized in the Jordan River, said:

> *The Spirit of the Lord is on me, because he has
> anointed me to proclaim good news to the poor.
> He has sent me to proclaim freedom for the pris-
> oners and recovery of sight to the blind, to set
> the oppressed free* (Luke 4:18).

Jesus is an example to believers still living on this earth.
The Bible says, "This is how love is made complete among
us so that we will have confidence on the day of judgment:
In this world we are like Jesus" (1 John 4:17). The same Holy
Spirit who anointed Jesus at the Jordan River was given to
us when we received the baptism of the Holy Spirit earlier in
this devotional. You are not some lowly worm in the dirt. You
are a child of God filled with the same Holy Spirit as Jesus
Christ. Just as God anointed Jesus, He has now anointed you

and sent you into this world. About the anointing of Jesus, the Bible says:

> How God anointed Jesus of Nazareth with the Holy Spirit and power, and how he went around doing good and healing all who were under the power of the devil, because God was with him (Acts 10:38).

This anointing from God applies to our gifts and passions. For example, I love sports, so whenever I played in a football game, I would confess over myself, "I am anointed to play football for the glory of God." One time, during halftime, one of my non-Christian teammates walked up to me and said he saw Jesus through the way I played. That is no coincidence. I challenge you to realize the gifts and passions you have and start confessing over your life that *you are anointed, and you are called.*

DECLARATION:

Father, thank You for giving me the special ability to live life for Your glory. Thank You for the breath in my lungs. Thank You for anointing me. Thank You for calling me. Greater are You, living inside me, than he who is in the world. Reveal to me today the gifts and passions that You want me to pursue. Open up my eyes so that I can see opportunities the way You see them. Open up my heart and eyes so that I can understand everything You are doing in my life. When people praise me, I will be sure to always praise You.

I am the light of the world. I have what the world so desperately needs.

Scripture Reading: Acts 10

DAY 29

STAY ON FIRE

I know your deeds, that you are neither cold nor hot. I
wish you were either one or the other! (Revelation 3:15)

Do you remember the passionate feeling—that joyful vibe—you have when you get done with church on Sunday or a summer camp or a solid time with the Lord? Nothing is better than being on fire for the Lord. God doesn't want us to just be on fire for Him sometimes. He wants us to live a burning life for Him *at all times.* Jesus said, in Revelation 3:15, "I know your deeds, that you are neither cold nor hot. I wish you were either one or the other!" When we are neither hot nor cold, we end up getting spewed out of God's mouth. This does not mean we no longer are saved or that God can't forgive us; it just means God ain't vibing with us when we are lukewarm.

The question is, what does it look like to live on fire for Jesus at all times? God has given each one of us gifts and passions. Some people try to cast them aside as unimportant and focus on worldly things and following others. But God wants you to use those gifts and passions and pursue them with all of your heart. For example, if someone really enjoys making music, but doesn't know Jesus yet, he will use his gifts to get better at making music for the world to enjoy. That is what it looks like to be cold. If someone who knows Jesus and is baptized in the Holy Spirit starts using her musical talents to spread the gospel and uplift people all across the world, that is what it looks like to be burning hot for the Lord. (I am not saying everyone needs to be a musician; I'm just using that one gift as an example.)

Whatever our gifts, we should give them to the Lord so that He can use us. Our gifts will make room for us and open doors of influence for us. When we do what He made us to do, we will have the greatest impact for Him. Success in life is not measured by the degrees we have, how much money we make, or our social status. Ultimate success is measured by what we have done with the gifts God gave us and what He told us to do.

DECLARATION:

Lord, please reveal Your plan for my life to me. Show me the gifts and passions You have given me. I choose to pursue You today. I choose to give You all my gifts and talents. I will change the world around me, because You live in me. I am anointed and gifted to _____ [insert your gift/passion]. I will never quit. I will fulfill my destiny.

Scripture Reading: Revelation 3

DAY 30

THE MIND OF CHRIST

For "who has known the mind of the Lord so as to instruct him?" But we have the mind of Christ (1 Corinthians 2:16).

Maybe you are a perfect student who loves every class and aces every test, but I needed Jesus at every step during middle and high school. What's so cool about God is that He doesn't just help us spiritually. He also wants to help us in this area of our lives. The Bible says, "For, 'Who has known the mind of the Lord so as to instruct him?' But we have the mind of Christ" (1 Cor. 2:16). Do not just accept your grades and your current mental ability. Do not just accept your current performance level at your job. When you gave your life to Christ, you received His ability. Do you think Jesus struggles with AP Chemistry? Do you really think God doesn't know the answers to Algebra? Do you think the Holy Spirit struggles to know the best way to do your job? You would be tripping if you think God needs to call for backup for your classes or job. Your friends and teachers and boss may not think you have the mind of Christ, but that doesn't matter.

When I was in high school, I was not the smartest kid, but I understood what the Bible says about me. If God said I had the mind of Christ, then I knew it was the truth. And I lived accordingly. To step into this perspective, you must choose to trust God over everything else you see in your life. When you believe you have the mind of Christ, your life will look drastically different. Instead of telling your friends you're going to fail the test, you will walk in confidence, knowing God has your back.

When you succeed in school and work, doing much better than you did before you knew Jesus, it will be an amazing testimony to God's goodness. By the end of my senior year, my principal called me and told me some crazy news: I was the valedictorian of more than four hundred students. I wasn't able to achieve that on my own. I was able to have that reward because I understood that I have the mind of Christ. I would be sure to do my best and leave the rest to God. Even when I felt like I didn't get a class or was having a tough time, I trusted that God would see me through. And He always did. When worry or fear tried to get on me, I refused because I knew that Jesus wouldn't worry about a small test.

I encourage you today to never quit. You are called and anointed and gifted. You have the blood of Jesus Christ. You have the mind of Christ. Whenever you are in school or work, set your goals high. Don't allow yourself to be brought down by feelings of worry and anxiety. Keep on pushing. Focus on little steps and you will find yourself higher than you have ever been before.

DECLARATION:

Father, thank You for giving me the mind of Christ. I refuse to worry about school or work. I will not worry about tests. I will not worry about grades. I am successful in school. I am successful in work. I will be successful with my grades. I am the light of the world. Everything I do is a testimony to Jesus living inside of me. I have the mind of Christ. I am not a failure. I am a success going places to succeed.

Scripture Reading: 1 Corinthians 2

Day 31

DON'T BE IN A RUSH

I waited patiently for the Lord to help me, and he turned to me and heard my cry (Psalm 40:1 NLT).

A few months ago, I was feeling very hungry one evening, and I knew I needed some good chicken in my belly. So I threw some frozen chicken into the air fryer and pulled it out thirty minutes later. When I cut it open, I saw that it was a little purple and black on the inside, and I felt uneasy about eating it. But instead of listening to common sense and putting it back in the air fryer, I chose to eat it all. I was so hungry that I had lost patience. Sure enough, late that night I started throwing up, and I spent the next two days with extreme salmonella. I learned a very valuable lesson that day: Preparation is *never* wasted time.

About this, David said, "I waited patiently for the Lord to help me, and he turned to me and heard my cry" (Ps. 40:1 NLT). The Bible tells us that many of the spiritual heroes we look to experienced seasons of waiting and preparation. Even Jesus Christ, the Son of God, waited thirty years to start His amazing ministry. In that time of waiting, He was getting ready and took joy in the process. He knew what was to come, and He grew in wisdom and understanding. If we want to fulfill our calling in God, we need to learn to wait patiently just like Jesus did.

Choose to start with what you have today and work with it instead of longing for what you don't yet have. Be faithful and smart with the things you already have, and God will reward you with more. You have an amazing life ahead of you. Take advantage of the time you have on this earth. A day is coming when you will be thankful you did what God called you to do. Don't allow yourself to get into sadness or disappointment with the things that haven't happened yet. Instead, choose to be thankful for what you already have.

When you were two years old, your parents had a good reason for not giving you a brand-new iPhone. You did not yet understand how to work technology in a safe way. Likewise, we are called to grow up and mature in who we are in Christ, in our spirit, our heart. We are called to grow up from being babies in Christ. Here's the thing: The way to grow up is to do something with what you already have. Find joy and get excited about what God is doing in your life right now. Stay patient and always prepare for the next season God has for you. Never quit because something hasn't worked out yet or you feel like it's taking too long. Trust God's timing, and keep doing what He tells you to do. When we love God, He will work out all things for our good.

DECLARATION:

Lord, thank You for today. Thank You for saving me. Jesus, thank You for pouring out Your blood on the cross for me. Thank You for the breath in my lungs. Thank You for giving me life. I choose to be faithful in what You have given me. I will do what You tell me to do. I am a child of God. I am called. I am anointed. I will fulfill my destiny. I will accomplish God's plan for my life. I can do all things through Christ who strengthens me. I will prepare for every step in my life.

Scripture Reading: Psalm 40

DAY 32

GET BOOED UP

But seek first his kingdom and his righteousness, and all these things will be given to you as well (Matthew 6:33).

Imagine that you have a girlfriend, but she starts hanging out with other guys and kissing them and posting them on her story. How do you think you would feel? If you are reasonable, you would say that's definitely out of pocket. If you have a relationship with someone, you expect them to be exclusively committed to you. When we say *yes* to Jesus, we get married to Him. This doesn't mean we can't talk to others, but it means Jesus wants to be first in our lives and to be with us everywhere we go. It is good to have friends and a significant other, but Jesus wants us to bring Him along. He wants to be part of every part of our lives.

Jesus said, in Matthew 6:33, "But seek first his kingdom and his righteousness, and all these things will be given to you as well." When you understand that you are married to Jesus, you will always leave room for Him, even when you are with someone else. (Especially leave room for Him if you're cuddling!) Not only that, but once you know you are in a relationship with Jesus, you will treat others differently. When a guy truly loves a girl, he will not see other girls in the same way that he sees *that one girl*. When we love Jesus, He will help us see others around us *His way*. Instead of thinking selfishly about how our friends and family can help us, we will instead think about how *we can help them*. Also, we will stop asking "Is this a sin?" and instead just live our lives wanting to please God every step of the way.

Nothing is as amazing as true love. Jesus Christ, author of the truest love story ever, has chosen and called us to Himself. Don't overlook His love. Don't overlook His sacrifice. Choose today to love Him back. A lot of Christian girls say, "I am dating Jesus," and it can be kinda cringe sometimes, but you know it really is true. We are actually married to Jesus, and that is how we should view everything. In every situation and relationship, we are called to be faithful to Him.

It's not hard to know whether an action hurts His heart. Many times, I have been in a situation or with a person, and I can just tell that something isn't right. I'm not always able to describe it in words, but it is most often a sense of uneasiness. When I get that uneasy feeling, I always know I need to pray and see what God wants me to do. That is called constant fellowship—or vibing—with Jesus. When we live like that, we will be tuned in to His heart and putting Him first in our lives.

DECLARATION:

Father, thank You for loving me. I choose to commit my life to You. I will not live a double life. I will not go anywhere without You. I will take You with me to every place I go. I do not want to hurt You. Help me to protect my heart. I ask You for wisdom for today in Jesus' name. I believe I receive it.

Scripture Reading: Matthew 6

DAY 33

THE SAME POWER

And if the Spirit of him who raised Jesus from the dead is living in you, he who raised Christ from the dead will also give life to your mortal bodies because of his Spirit who lives in you (Romans 8:11).

Smith Wigglesworth was an evangelist in the late 1800s and early 1900s, and he was a wild guy. One time, he walked into a funeral to find the dead body surrounded by people crying and mourning. To everyone's shock, Wigglesworth took the body out of the open casket and slammed it against the wall. He said, "In the name of Jesus Christ, walk!" The body fell lifeless to the floor. He picked it up again and said, "In the name of Jesus Christ, walk!" Again, the body fell to the floor. For the third time, he grabbed the body and threw it against the wall, shouting, *"I said, 'In the name of Jesus Christ of Nazareth, walk!'"* Sure enough, the man came back to life, took a huge breath, and stood up and walked. He was raised from the dead. Wigglesworth would go on to raise at least thirteen other people from the dead. He understood what the Bible says in Romans 8:11:

> *And if the Spirit of him who raised Jesus from the dead is living in you, he who raised Christ from*

the dead will also give life to your mortal bodies because of his Spirit who lives in you.

The resurrection of Jesus from the dead is not just a cool story. It is a living example for believers that we can live a powerful life. Our Savior isn't dead; *He's alive.* Not even death is more powerful than Jesus Christ. But this resurrection power isn't just for Jesus; it is also for us. That same resurrection power now lives in you. If you become sick, confess over yourself that you have resurrection power living on the inside. When you are struggling to get something done in school or to find the motivation you need, believe that you have resurrection power living on the inside.

Some people might think it's crazy to believe that the same power that raised Jesus from the dead now dwells in us—but that is exactly what the Bible says. You might wonder, "Gabe, does that mean I never have to die?" Well, here is the thing: We can only believe God for what He says. Even though we have resurrection power living in us, we still have a limited amount of time here on earth before we go to heaven. But if something happens and it's looking like we might be leaving this earth early, we can absolutely believe in God to keep us alive.

DECLARATION:

Father, I thank You that Jesus lives inside of me. I have resurrection power dwelling on the inside. The same Spirit that raised Jesus from the dead now lives in me. Greater is He who lives in me than he who is in the world. Nothing is impossible for God. All things are possible.

Scripture Reading: Romans 8

BUILT DIFFERENT

DAY 34

AN ALLIGATOR PRANK

Then Jesus said to his disciples, "Whoever wants to be my disciple must deny themselves and take up their cross and follow me" (Matthew 16:24).

Recently, I went hiking at a park close to my house with my friend Zach. Along the way, we figured we would jump into the lake. I had heard that alligators live in the lake, but I had never seen one. Sure enough, when we got to the place where we were going to jump in, we saw two carcasses; one looked like a baby alligator. We laughed it off and got into the lake. I should have known right away that something was sketchy, because it felt like a swamp, and my feet kept getting stuck to the bottom. We were about thirty feet from the shore when Zach said, "Gabe, there's a gator right here." I looked toward him, and I saw two eyes sticking out of the water. I swam toward shore faster than I ever had before. As I was booking it out of there, Zach was a little behind me trying to get his shoes. I kept yelling at him, telling him it's better to lose his shoes than to lose his life.

We both ended up being OK, but I will never get back in that lake. Later, I found out that Zach had been playing a prank on me and hadn't really seen an alligator. Of course, if the alligator had been real, Zach needed to learn a lesson that day about what was more important—his shoes or his life. (They were Crocs, so I guess some people would say his shoes were very important.) Regardless, you can replace a pair of shoes—even Crocs—at the store, but you can't buy a new leg (at least, not a real one). In that moment, Zach needed to count the cost. He had to sacrifice a temporary thing (his Crocs) for a more lasting one (his life).

Similarly, Jesus told His disciples, "Whoever wants to be my disciple must deny themselves and take up their cross and follow me" (Matt. 16:24). When we choose to follow Jesus, we must lay down our selfish desires and fleshly wants. Right now, how much money you have or how cute your crush is or how many Instagram followers you have might seem like a big deal, but they are temporary compared to the eternal life we will live with God. Every day, we are called to crucify the flesh and love others. When we choose to love, our actions will have eternal significance.

DECLARATION:

Jesus, I choose to follow You. I will crucify my flesh today. I choose to love others just like You love me. Help me to understand the eternal weight of my actions. Open my eyes so that I can know what is important to You. Help me to spend my time correctly. Help me to focus on Your plan for my life.

Scripture Reading: Matthew 16

DAY 35

STOP WEARING A MASK

Let us then approach God's throne of grace with confidence, so that we may receive mercy and find grace to help us in our time of need (Hebrews 4:16).

I realize my title might be controversial in the days of COVID mask requirements, but that's not what I'm talking about here. Regardless of the reasons one might have for wearing a mask in public, we can all agree that masks hide people's emotions from others. Masks provide a way for people to hide behind something. But many people, Christians included, don't need a physical mask to hide behind; they have learned to wear a spiritual mask to prevent others from knowing how they really are doing. Too many of us know how to fake our outward appearance to mask our true emotions. But when I have friends over to my apartment, I want them to come the way they really are. I want to see the real them, not a masked "perfect" version.

God also wants us to come to Him in honesty. We can't play games with church or worship. God doesn't want fake children. He wants the real you. With God, you never have to fear whether He will accept you. God isn't going to view your life and say, "Guess you just aren't good enough." Instead, when you come to Him honestly, He will love your humility and help you through the changes you need. The Bible says,

"Let us then approach God's throne of grace with confidence, so that we may receive mercy and find grace to help us in our time of need" (Heb. 4:16).

My pastor once told me that a lot of young people do not go to the front of the church on Sunday morning because they made some bad mistakes on Saturday night. But he said that the altar is the *perfect* place for them, because it is where they can get close to God. Even if you messed up a lot the night before, you can do nothing better than worship God with all your heart the next morning. The mercies of the Lord are new every morning. God is always faithful to forgive and wash you clean. You are His child no matter what, and you can always boldly come into His presence.

DECLARATION:

Lord, today I choose to take off the mask. I approach Your throne with the real me. I want to know You more. I humble myself and repent of all sin. Jesus, I love You. Help me to be more upfront with those around me. If I have deception or dishonesty in my life, reveal it to me. Thank You for being real to me. Show me the people You want me to be accountable to. Thank You for sending me more Christian friends. I will be the one to love and stay real.

Scripture Reading: Hebrews 4

DAY 36

STAY PREPARED

And behold, I am coming quickly, and My reward is with Me, to give to every one according to his work (Revelation 22:12 NKJV).

I f you had a date tonight, would you wait until the last moment to get ready? Even though that is how you may treat school or even chores, when it comes to something like a date, you better be prepared. If you really like that person, you have to show that you are taking the relationship seriously. Just like we would take a date seriously, we should also take God seriously. God is a lot of fun. I'm not saying we need to have serious faces all the time. But when you really love someone, you will be sure to be prepared for whatever that person needs from you.

In the Bible, Jesus said, "And behold, I am coming quickly, and My reward is with Me, to give to every one according to his work" (Rev. 22:12 NKJV). When Jesus comes back, we can't be caught lacking. God has a plan for your life that He wants to get started with *today*. If the devil can't get you off track, he will convince you that God's plan can wait until tomorrow. Procrastination will steal God's plan for your life. Waiting one day will turn into a week and then a month and then a year. We all have had those English papers that were due in a month and then all of a sudden it's 11:50 PM the night before it's due, and we are only halfway done. Don't procrastinate on the plan of God.

Our flesh will lead us to believe that temporary things matter most. It is easy to get caught up in work, making more money, dating, and so forth. But instead of being fleshly minded, we have been called to be spiritually minded, which means focusing on the gospel and love. Even when we are spending time in school or work or in the world, we can do our best and believe that God is using us to reach others. If you have an urge in your heart to start doing something for God, don't wait. Don't feel like you need all the official endorsement of all your friends to do what God told you to do. Faith starts by taking one step. In each step, God will prove Himself faithful to you.

DECLARATION:

Lord, I am excited for Your return. Help me to become ready for the end. Help me to spread this gospel so that the world can know how much You love them. Reveal to me any areas of my life where I have procrastinated. If I have been slow to answer You, I repent. I want to be fast to listen and obey. I am quick to hear Your voice. I am quick to obey.

Scripture Reading: Revelation 22

DAY 37

TRUE LOVE

Father, forgive them, for they do not know
what they do (Luke 23:34 NKJV).

Anyone scrolling through TikTok or other social media will notice the number of couple videos out there. Young people all across the world are focused on finding "true love." Everyone has fantasies and dreams of finding "the one." I hate to break it to you, but those dreams will let you down. No one can love you quite like Jesus can. Human love will always fall short compared to the God kind of love. Don't get me wrong: It is not bad to desire to be loved. No one wants to be alone in this world, and God made us with the desire for human love and fellowship. God wants us to be together and not separate. But a lot of times we go seeking for the God kind of love in places outside of God.

When two believers who are on fire for God get married, it is amazing, because they have God at the center of it all. The strongest type of rope is one that has three strands. When you choose to marry someone and put Jesus at the center, He strengthens each side of the covenant. The point is: Whether you are single or married, you should always rely first on Jesus. Also, when your source is God and not people, you will pull less on people, and they will feel free around you, because your expectations do not make them feel like they must measure up.

God's love for us is unconditional, and because of that, we can unconditionally love others even when they do us wrong. Some people think they should only be kind and loving to their friends or people they like, but true love makes sacrifices for those who don't deserve it. Do you think, when Jesus died on the cross, that He only shed His blood for the nice churchgoing Christians? No. Jesus died for *all* people, including those who crucified Him. That is why He said, "Father, forgive them, for they do not know what they do" (Luke 23:34 NKJV). As Christians, we are called to walk in that same spirit of forgiveness and love.

DECLARATION:

Father God, thank You for loving me. Your love is unconditional. I am loved. I am chosen. The creator of the universe has chosen to call me His child. I am a child of the Most High God. I am forgiven. Lord, help me to love others just like You love me. Give me Your eyes. I choose to forgive others. I forgive every person for every wrong against me. I will not carry offense or bitterness. I release all bitterness from my soul in Jesus' name.

Scripture Reading: Luke 23

DAY 38

REFUSING TO BE OFFENDED

A person's wisdom yields patience; it is one's
glory to overlook an offense (Proverbs 19:11).

A big difference exists between protecting yourself from toxic people and carrying the spirit of offense and bitterness. If someone throws a punch at you, you need to defend yourself however you can. But if someone trash-talks your shoes or talks about you behind your back, true strength will be able to disregard these offenses. Attention is like a currency. When you choose to place your attention on a matter, you are saying it is valuable. Sometimes you do need to focus on something negative in order to stay safe or to save someone, but generally speaking, many people get caught up in things they shouldn't because their feelings have been hurt.

It will *always* be your choice whether you allow words and people to bring you down. As the Bible says, "A person's wisdom yields patience; it is one's glory to overlook an offense" (Prov. 19:11). Spiritually immature people will allow words to bring them down. It's time to grow spiritually so that we understand that when people reject us, it means very little, because we always have God's support. If you are touchy or quick to be offended, you are missing out on God's best for you.

Recently, a friend and I drove to Chipotle. When we pulled into the parking lot, a large white truck was pulling out and then stopped. As my friend kept going, the other driver got visibly angry, pushed the gas, and started chasing us. We were a couple feet away from getting rammed. Thankfully, we drove away and everything ended OK, but it reminded me how sad it is to see people get offended so quickly by little things. Life just isn't fun when you hold bitterness about other people's actions. If you believe your life is a result of how other people have treated you, your mindset needs to change. Yes, I am sure that people *have* wronged you. We live in a fallen world, and wrongs happen to everyone. But you have a choice as to how you will respond. You always have a chance to *win* by choosing to walk in love. That doesn't necessarily mean you will get "your way." Instead, it means you will go God's way by forgiving and moving on, regardless of how the details of the situation work out.

DECLARATION:

Father, thank You for loving me. I choose to live unoffended. I am not touchy or fretful. God, I thank You for Your approval. You have my back. I will not have expectations from people that only You can handle. Help me to keep my heart safe. Show me areas of my life where I have misplaced my attention. I want to focus on the things You want me to focus on.

Scripture Reading: Proverbs 19

DAY 39

FULL SEND

"Lord, if it's you," Peter replied, "tell me to come to you on the water. "Come," he said (Matthew 14:28–29).

Recently, I traveled to Austin, TX, to go cliff jumping. After a three-hour drive, we found the spot by the river. As we were chilling and making jokes at the top of the cliff, out of the corner of my eye, I saw a body plop right off the cliff. To my shock, I realized my friend Chase had just fully sent himself to the water. He ended up being just fine. In fact, he had the best landing of the day. At first I was like, *Man, this guy is tripping!* But after realizing everything had worked out for him, I saw that his choice was actually wise. After he took one look down the cliff and saw where he needed to go, he didn't let any questions or doubt pull him down. He went full-send mode into the water.

God has called all of us to have a full-send faith mode. When God says something and tells us to go somewhere, we must not allow questions and doubt to enter in. Wisdom will look ahead and understand the next step, but after that, we have to just trust that God will look after us and believe He knows what's best. When I was running off that cliff into the water, a thousand thoughts entered my mind. So many times, I felt like stopping and just chickening out. But thankfully, I too just got a running start and went right over the ledge into the water. It was so worth it.

We see an example of this in Peter's response when Jesus was walking on the water. "'Lord, if it's you,' Peter replied, 'tell me to come to you on the water.' 'Come,' he said" (Matt. 14:28). Before Peter took that step, he had a choice. He could have stayed in the boat and never walked on the water. Instead, he chose to go full-send mode, and he walked on water that day. The point here is not that you should jump off cliffs or try to walk on water, but instead, that you are called to apply this principle of going full send to your faith walk.

When God calls you to talk to a stranger and tell that person about Jesus, it may seem impossible. But full-send faith will know that you have nothing to lose. Don't be afraid to do what God tells you to do. Trust that His words will guide you and protect you. You will always be safe when you are moving on God's word.

DECLARATION:

I trust the word of God. I trust in what God tells me to do. I will take a leap of faith every day. I will not place my eyes on distractions. I will focus on the task at hand. I will fix my eyes on Jesus. I will not allow doubt to stay in my heart. I will fill my heart with faith and love. Jesus, I trust You.

Scripture Reading: Matthew 14

DAY 40

WE GOT BEEF WITH THE DEVIL

Love never fails... (1 Corinthians 13:8).

Life in high school was pretty crazy, especially because at my school we would have a couple fights happening every week. Girls would be pulling hair and screaming, and the crowds would gather for entertainment. What always confused me was what the fights were actually about. The majority of the time, they were as meaningless as how one person looked at another person or a Snapchat comment about one of their looks. They were beefin' (fighting) for all the wrong reasons.

When we give our lives to Christ, we are called out of beefin' with people and into beefin' with the devil. I will never forget a testimony I received from a young man in California. He said:

> If it wasn't for your videos, I wouldn't be born again and love Jesus. I went out yesterday and saw a guy I was beefing with and was ready to go whoop his butt, but then I thought about that Jesus wouldn't want me fighting, so thanks to Jesus and your videos.

The Bible talks about this in Ephesians 6:12,

For our struggle is not against flesh and blood, but against the rulers, against the authorities, against the powers of this dark world and against the spiritual forces of evil in the heavenly realms.

As humans, we have a fleshly tendency to get angry and blame others. But we must identify the real enemy: the devil. He is the one who works through people to try to get under our skin. Then he will blame the people involved—or blame us—and he makes his exit unnoticed. His time of getting away untouched is over. Make a choice today to quit beefin' with people and have beef with the true enemy: Satan. You don't have to be "good enough" to beat him up. Jesus has already defeated him and given us the keys to the kingdom. Now we just enforce that victory.

Refuse to be offended when others wrong you. Trust that God will protect you and be your defender. When you love others like God does, you are crushing the kingdom of darkness. As the Bible says, "Love never fails..." (1 Cor. 13:8). Nothing can stop you when you are walking in God's love.

DECLARATION:

Lord, I thank You for the victory You won on the cross. You defeated the grave and the pits of hell. I do not wrestle against flesh and blood. People are not my problem. Help me to understand what is truly going on around me. Help me to not get angry at others. Show me how to walk in the love that You have called me to. Thank You for being my defender. Thank You for protecting me. I don't have to get back at people, because You have my back.

Scripture Reading: Ephesians 6

DAY 41

STAY IN GOD'S BLESSING

I am the true vine, and my Father is the gardener (John 15:1).

If you had a winning lottery ticket and all you had to do was go to the gas station to claim the prize, would it be logical to visit Burger King expecting to receive the money there? You would be crazy if you thought that. You have to go to a specific location to get the money you won.

The same is true in our spiritual walk. Jesus said:

> *I am the true vine, and my Father is the gardener. He cuts off every branch in me that bears no fruit, while every branch that does bear fruit he prunes so that it will be even more fruitful. You are already clean because of the words I have spoken to you. Remain in me, as I also remain in you. No branch can bear fruit by itself; it must remain in the vine. Neither can you bear fruit unless you remain in me* (John 15:1–4).

God has an amazing plan for your life that is better than winning the lottery, but the key to having God's blessing is remaining in the place where He has called you. You cannot expect Him to help you if you disobey His commands. So many people blame God for their problems even though they aren't living for Him. When I played football, every year during the first week of summer camp, everyone wished they had been in the weight room the months before. But by the time we were running up and down the field in practice, it was too late.

In our walk with God, we should not wait until Sunday to get our lives right before Him. The way to stay in God's blessing is to always be in tune with Him, to always be willing to change and repent. We are not called to just repent once and then everything is great. Instead, we are called to have a humble heart and repent as soon as we know we have walked the wrong way. The good news is, God always forgives us and washes us clean when we repent. The Bible says, "If we confess our sins, he is faithful and just and will forgive us our sins and purify us from all unrighteousness" (1 John 1:9). I want to encourage you today that you can always trust God in bringing everything to him. He is not angry at you or holding your faults against you. He always responds in love. The blood of Jesus is thicker than your mistakes.

DECLARATION:

Father God, thank You for blessing me with life and breath today. I humble myself and repent of all sin. If anything is pulling me away from You, please reveal it to me. Jesus, I want to be closer to You today. I choose to stay in the blessing. I choose to shut all the doors I have previously opened to the devil. Help me to keep my eyes and ears clean from worldly influence. God, when You speak to me, I will obey.

Scripture Reading: John 15

DAY 42

KNOW YOUR WORTH

For you know that it was not with perishable things such as silver or gold that you were redeemed from the empty way of life handed down to you from your ancestors, but with the precious blood of Christ, a lamb without blemish or defect (1 Peter 1:18–19).

Lebron James would never say *yes* to working a minimum wage job flipping burgers at McDonald's. He knows his time is much better spent playing basketball and making millions of dollars. He knows his time is worth a certain amount of money, and he won't accept less than that amount. *Forbes* may assign people a value based on their net worth, but the truth is that every person is worth much more than a dollar sign could ever signify. We are literally worth the blood of Jesus Christ. The Bible says:

For you know that it was not with perishable things such as silver or gold that you were redeemed from the empty way of life handed down to you from your ancestors, but with the precious blood of Christ, a lamb without blemish or defect (1 Peter 1:18–19).

Your ultimate net value is not found in how much money you make or the successes or failures of your life. Your value is found in the price God paid for you. When you know how much God loves and accepts you, you will not be affected by people who reject you. Imagine that I have a crush who I want to ask out. One day, I finally get up the courage to ask her out, and she says *yes*. But later in the day, a super cringe girl tells me she doesn't find me attractive. Would I let the second girl's opinion of me change my mood? No way—I would laugh, because my crush has already accepted me, and this other girl's opinion can hold no weight compared to that. This is how we need to be with God's approval.

When we choose to love God with our whole heart and place Him first, we will live in a constant joyful energy rooted in His acceptance of us. We won't be so clingy to people, trying to get their approval. Instead, we will live with confidence, knowing that the creator of the universe has chosen to call us His children. When the devil puts thoughts of insecurity inside your head, refuse to listen and kick them out. *Ain't nobody got time for that.* Run back to the words of our loving Father who calls us His beloved. We are the apple of His eye. His thoughts about us are more numerous than the sand on the seashore.

DECLARATION:

I am the apple of God's eye. I am His peculiar treasure. I am worth the blood of Jesus. My past does not define me. My success does not define me. The love of Jesus Christ defines me. I am a new creation and the righteousness of God in Christ. I am forgiven. I am loved. I am accepted. I am chosen. I am anointed. I am special. God lives inside of me. I do not need people's approval. I am not rejected. I am accepted in the beloved.

Scripture Reading: 1 Peter 1

BUILT DIFFERENT

DAY 43

DON'T WASTE TIME

Redeeming the time, because the days are evil (Ephesians 5:16 NKJV).

No matter how much money you earn in your lifetime, you will never be able to buy more time. And even if you are not a millionaire, you are rich in time. A lot of young people say things like, "I would serve God, but right now I just want to have fun and live it up." And they think, for some reason, they can wait until they are seventy, sitting in a chair and watching the news, to fully give their lives to serving God. They think everything will just work out fine that way. But God has a plan for each one of us starting *today*. Besides, it is so much more fun to live for Him now and not wait until later. The Bible says:

> *As God's co-workers we urge you not to receive God's grace in vain. For he says, "In the time of my favor I heard you, and in the day of salvation I helped you." I tell you, now is the time of God's favor, now is the day of salvation* (2 Corinthians 6:1–2).

If we waste time by following after only temporary pleasures, we will have so much regret at the end of our lives. You might say, "But no matter what, I'm still saved, so what does it matter, Gabe?" Here's the thing: Even though your salvation is secure, the reward you will get in heaven is based on the life you live here on earth.

Also, people around you don't yet know Jesus, but if you're just out living for the world, how will they hear the gospel? What kind of example will you be? Your walk with God doesn't just affect you. The world around us is watching us to see if God is real or if it is just an act. When we live pure lives before Him and walk in His blessing, they can't help but realize the love that Jesus has for them too. About this, Jesus said:

> That all of them may be one, Father, just as you are in me and I am in you. May they also be in us so that the world may believe that you have sent me (John 17:21).

Make a choice today that you won't waste time, but will follow wholeheartedly after God. The world is counting on you to not quit. Let's show them that life with Jesus is a lot greener than life on the other side.

DECLARATION:

Lord, I thank You for the time You have given me on earth. Help me to not waste time. Help me to be faithful with what You have given me. Thank You for my family and friends. Show me areas of my life in which I have been unproductive. I have a strong work ethic. I will persevere. If I fall, I will get back up again. I choose not to complain. I choose to be thankful. I will always take responsibility for my actions. Thank You, Lord, for Your grace.

Scripture Reading: John 17

DAY 44

WALKING IN GOD'S PEACE

*Let not your heart be troubled; you believe in
God, believe also in Me* (John 14:1 NKJV).

M any people think they need to be problem-free in
order to have peace in life. Maybe you think that
when summer comes around and you have a break
from school or work, then life will be chill. But as you get older,
you will realize this is a false hope. True peace is not found
through avoiding the storm. True peace comes from walking
with God even in the midst of the storm. When Jesus and
His disciples were trapped in a storm they thought would kill
them, Jesus was literally sleeping in the back of the boat. He
was sleeping *while the storm was raging*. If you wait to walk
in the peace of God until your problems disappear, you will
never have peace in life. In high school, I always thought that
once I graduated, life would become way easier, and I would
not worry again. That thinking wasn't true at all. Problems
are present in every season of life.

But our problems don't have to impact our peace. We
can have the peace of God today. The Bible says,

> *Do not be anxious about anything, but in every
> situation, by prayer and petition, with thanksgiv-
> ing, present your requests to God. And the peace*

of God, which transcends all understanding, will
guard your hearts and your minds in Christ Jesus
(Philippians 4:6).

This scripture says it is our choice whether we will walk in the peace of God. This doesn't mean we can be lazy with our lives or just not focus on what is going on around us. Instead, it means we can have the faith response in any circumstance. Through prayer and petition, with thanksgiving, we can bring everything that tries to bring us down to God. When we choose to be thankful in the midst of the storm, we will start walking in the peace He has for us.

You may say, "But, Gabe, what if I have anxiety attacks, and I just fall into worry?" A doctor may have diagnosed you with an anxiety disorder, but Jesus is your healer, and He has another word for you. Jesus has promised that you can have His peace at all times. There are no addendums or excuses to the promises of God. Many of things we identify with and have been diagnosed with are not permanent disorders; rather, they are things we have allowed to enter into our lives and chosen to accept because it's "who we are." Who you are is now rooted in Christ Jesus, and you now have what He has. Last time I checked, He does not struggle with an anxiety disorder. Neither should you. I say this in love! I don't want you to feel condemnation or guilt, but to know that you are truly free in Jesus' name. Let His peace rule in your life.

DECLARATION:
Jesus, thank You for giving me Your peace that
passes all understanding. I refuse to accept worry

and anxiety. I do not get anxiety attacks. I attack the devil through the power of Jesus Christ. I am not on the defense; I'm on the offense. I choose to walk in the rest of God. I'm not stressing, because I know Jesus has my back. God has me in the palm of His hand. I am safe in His hand. I don't have to fear. God will take care of me. I cast all my worries on You, Lord, for I know You care for me.

Scripture Reading: Philippians 4

DAY 45

FULLY COMMIT

Looking unto Jesus, the author and finisher
of our faith... (Hebrews 12:2 NKJV).

Recently, I went to a water park in Texas that has a for-ty-foot slide that launches you into the air. For some reason, I thought it would be cool if I tried a backflip, because I figured, *What's the worst that could happen?* Sure, I could have fractured my face and been flown to the ER, but hey, you only live once, right? So as I was going down the slide, I realized I actually had never done a backflip before in my life. When I launched off the slide, I started the rotation, but then I chickened out and didn't fully commit to the flip. I ended up turning and flailing and smacking my butt. Because I chickened out, I wasn't able to complete the flip. You may think I am lame for that, but more importantly, we have all bailed on God more times than we realize.

Imagine you are having lunch with your friends at school, and you feel a slight urge in your heart to talk to a person who is sitting alone. At first you think you might go over there, but then you remember that you don't want to embarrass yourself in front of others and ruin your cool reputation, so you just stay seated. The lunch ends, and as you walk away with your friends, that person who was sitting alone drags him- or herself back to class alone. You thought you were just "saving your reputation," but that slight urge in your heart was most likely God wanting you to love on and be a friend to the person who needed it most that day. Because you got afraid and bailed before doing what God told you to do, nothing happened.

I want to encourage you to never bail on God. When you first start obeying Him and taking that step, it will be challenging. It will feel like it's impossible. You will start to have second thoughts, and doubt will fill your head. But just keep walking forward. Keep believing that when God is leading you to do something, He will help you finish it. That's why the Bible says we are "looking unto Jesus, the author and finisher of our faith" (Heb. 12:2 NKJV). You may not be able to finish a backflip every time, but Jesus will help you finish whatever you need to finish in life. Just don't bail on Him. God doesn't create quitters.

DECLARATION:

Father God, I thank You for giving me boldness. When You speak, I will obey. I trust the words of the Lord. I trust the word of God. I have a full-send mentality. I am not a loser. I am not a quitter. I will not stop halfway. I will finish my course and run my race. I will not be affected by the opinions of people. I have been fully accepted by God. I will be faithful to God in every area of my life.

Scripture Reading: Hebrews 12

PEOPLE: GOD'S MOST PRIZED POSSESSION

Whoever is not with me is against me, and whoever does not gather with me scatters (Matthew 12:30).

Earlier in this devotional, we learned that we are worth the blood of Jesus. You know that you are built different because of Jesus, and you know you aren't the only one Jesus died for. God doesn't just want a family of one child; Jesus gave Himself so that He could have as many children as the stars in the sky. Culture tries to convince us that certain companies or bitcoins or items are the most valuable assets in the world. But *people* will always be the most valuable. When I was in high school, it was so easy to get caught up with getting good grades for myself or talking to a pretty girl or improving my football skills, but in reality, God's best plan was right beside me in the friends and teachers and students who walked the halls with me every day. Grades and sports and girls are somewhat important, but in the ultimate picture, those things will fade away.

What *is* eternal is the lives of those around us. Whether we like it or not, everyone is either going to heaven or hell. We aren't getting reincarnated as some big hippo or ice freezing indefinitely. This means that where we go after we die really matters. What is important to God should also be important to us. Because we know we are the apple of God's eye, we should also be willing to see others as the apple of His eye. Because we know how much God values us and calls us precious, we should be willing to sacrifice ourselves for others with His love. When the Bible says, in Matthew 6, to "seek first the kingdom," it doesn't mean you should polish a church building all day. Instead, it means you should put others above yourself.

Your ultimate destiny will not be found by trying to advance your own goals and desires. Instead, it will happen when you use your gifts and talents to help the people around you. There is only one you, and you are the one the world needs. (They need the Jesus Christ in you—the greater one.) If you struggle to know that you are loved and precious in God's sight, you will struggle to love others. But when you know how much you are loved, it will be easy to let that flow from you everywhere you go.

DECLARATION:

Lord, what is important to You is important to me. Help me to see people through Your eyes. Help me to keep my priorities in line. I want to seek Your kingdom first. I will put others ahead of me. I will work for others before working for me. My dreams and pursuits will have the good of others in mind. Jesus, I love You.

Scripture Reading: Matthew 12

DAY 47

KNOWING GOD

*Now Adam knew Eve his wife, and
she conceived...* (Genesis 4:1 NKJV).

H ave you ever had a family member or friend tell you they "know" a celebrity only to find out they barely saw that celebrity's make-up artist's sister's cousin at a Friday night baseball game? It's always funny to me how quickly people claim they know others when they barely do. Think about how God must feel when many Christians claim to know Him, but their lives tell a different story. To *know* someone does not mean you've talked to them before or met them once. When the Bible talks about knowing someone, that means a deep, intimate relationship. The Bible even uses the word *knew* to talk about when Adam slept with Eve and she became pregnant. To know someone means to go deeper than a surface-level relationship. It takes intentional effort and time to know someone for who they really are. It is not hard to know about someone; it is completely different to *know* that person.

Today, no matter how much you know about God, it is time to *know Him.* Spend some extra time worshiping Him. Thank Him for everything He has done for you. Get alone in your closet or a space where no one else is and just spend time with Him. It is important to set aside any distractions, especially your phone, because your notifications will get you sidetracked quickly. When you spend alone time with God, you will get to know Him more and more. Nothing is stopping your pursuit of God except you. You never have to question whether God will be there, accept you, or still love you after you mess up. You can always be confident that He will show up for you because He *knows* you and loves you.

In relationships, it can be tough sometimes to know if a person wants to hang out with you. Some people can be super indirect. Instead of telling you they don't want to hang out, they just give excuse after excuse for why they can't make it. No one likes to be on the receiving end of that. The good news is, God is a lot better than those indirect people. He is perfectly straightforward about how He feels about you, and He always wants to be with you. You never have to fear that God will send mixed signals. His intentions are clear: He wants you. So spend some quiet time in prayer and worship with Him today.

DECLARATION:

Father, I want to know You more today. I don't just want to know about You. I don't just want to hear about You. I want to know You person-ally. I want to know You for who You really are. I trust that Your intentions are clear. I trust that Your heart is deep. Show me Your glory. Reveal Your heart to me. Let's hang out today. Let's vibe. I worship You and praise You, for You are good, and Your mercy endures forever.

Scripture Reading: Philippians 3

DAY 48

STAY CHARGED UP

But you, beloved, building yourselves up on your most holy faith, praying in the Holy Spirit (Jude 1:20 NKJV).

Some people wait until their phone is at 2 percent charge and then they desperately scramble for a charger, taking their sibling's charger and causing all hell to break loose. (I may be that type of person, but for the sake of this illustration, we're just going to assume it's your little sister.) You don't need to be a rocket scientist to know that you shouldn't wait until your phone is at 1 percent to start charging it again. The best way to manage your phone's charge is to stay at a stable charge. Not only does this enable you to have a working phone when you need it, but it also keeps you from losing your mind and your relationship with your siblings over a charger.

Just as we need to keep our phones charged, even more importantly, we need to keep our relationship with God *charged up.* It's been a couple weeks since we talked about tongues, and now it's time again. I will never run out of words to say about tongues. The Bible says,

> *But you, beloved, building yourselves up on your most holy faith, praying in the Holy Spirit, keep yourselves in the love of God, looking for the*

mercy of our Lord Jesus Christ unto eternal life (Jude 1:20–21 NKJV).

The way we build our spiritual charge is by praying in the Holy Spirit, or praying in tongues. Praying in the Holy Spirit is not some advanced spiritual technique reserved for pastors. It is the prayer language gift that is given to all believers and that we can all freely walk in. A person's spirit, which the Bible describes as the inner person or inner man, joins with the Holy Spirit, and as the person's tongue and throat move, words of heavenly languages (tongues) will flow out. The more you pray in tongues, the more you will charge up your relationship with God. Whenever I pray in tongues, I am way more likely to be kind toward others and to behave more like God. That is not a coincidence!

Going to church once a week or even reading the Bible once a day will not make us spiritual giants. Tongues is a spiritual gift and strategy from heaven to help us stay charged up and grow spiritually. Smith Wigglesworth once said, "I don't often spend more than half an hour in prayer at one time, but I never go more than half an hour without praying." While it is important to quiet your mind and spend time with God, God also wants you to take Him with you throughout your whole day. Remember, this is not a religion. This isn't once-a-week Christianity. This is living with your best friend every day of your life.

Now spend some time in prayer. Open up your mouth by faith and pray in tongues. Even if it doesn't feel like anything or it just sounds like mutters, don't be afraid. Keep moving your mouth and let her rip!

DECLARATION:

Father, thank You for my prayer language. Thank You for sending the Holy Spirit to me so that I can pray in tongues. I choose today to charge myself up in the Holy Spirit. As an act of my will, I pray in tongues today. Jesus, thank You for baptizing me in the Holy Spirit and fire.

Scripture Reading: Jude 1

DAY 49

GREEN GRASS

He makes me to lie down in green pastures (Psalm 23:2 NKJV).

Have you ever looked at your neighbor's grass during the summer, when it's dry and brown, and realized that your grass is better? Maybe you're thinking, *Absolutely not, Gabe. That is weird, bro.* But I grew up mowing lawns, so I think about quirky stuff like that. And I was grateful that my family took care of the house and yard, because some of our neighbors' houses looked ratchet. We can compare yard-care standards in my neighborhood to people-care standards in the spiritual realm.

When you enter into God's family, He will take much better care of you than the world ever could. In the Psalms, David wrote, "The Lord is my shepherd; I shall not want. He makes me to lie down in green pastures; He leads me beside the still waters. He restores my soul..." (Ps. 23:1–3 NKJV). God is the best person to follow. The devil will place thoughts in your head like, *Wouldn't it be better if I just had sex now instead of waiting until marriage? What's the worst that could happen?* Or, *Don't worry about how that will affect your family. Do it because you want to. Take that drink. Smoke some of that up.* He will try to convince you that living in the world is more fun than living for God. No matter how strong in our faith we think we are, while we live on earth we *all* face thoughts like this. The devil always tries to convince us the grass is greener on the other side. But it's simply not true.

God is the one who invented fun. The devil just perverts it. The devil is not creative and cannot create anything good. Sadly, he has the majority of the world convinced that living in sin will be better than living for Jesus. The truth is: When you live for Christ, you will have the *most fun* because He invented fun. To overcome those thoughts of comparison and the temptation to pursue sin, run back to your first love: Jesus Christ. *Remember* all the good things He has done for you—the sins He forgave and the eternal salvation He purchased for you. Remember that He is making a mansion for you in heaven, and you never have to fear going to hell. When you have no fear of death, you will be able to truly live. As you stir yourself up about all the good things God has done for you, your eyes will open, and those evil thoughts will fall to the ground.

DECLARATION:

God, thank You for bringing me into Your home. I trust that the grass will always be greener on Your side, God. You are the most fun. I refuse to allow thoughts of comparison and doubt to stay in my mind. I choose instead to remember all the good things You have done for me. I remember the salvation You purchased for me on that cross. I thank You that I don't have to fear hell anymore. I thank You for the joy of the Holy Spirit.

Scripture Reading: Galatians 5

DAY 50

DON'T BE HAVING DEVIL BREATH

...He who is in you is greater than he who
is in the world (1 John 4:4 NKJV).

A while ago, my roommate, Nik, and I visited a church in the Dallas area. Admittedly, we were on the lookout for girls (not an action I necessarily endorse, but it is the truth in this story). Midway through the service, Nik looked at me and said, "Bruh, your breath is horrible. I can smell it from all the way over here." I didn't believe him, even after he told me again later in the service. When the service ended, as we were walking out, two girls came up to us, and we started talking to them. One of them asked Nik for his number, so I guess the day was a *win* for him. For me, not so much.

As I was talking with one of the girls, she started backing up, and her facial expression said: *I need to get away from this guy!* For the first time since middle school, I did not feel confident talking to a girl. Then it finally clicked in my mind—*she doesn't want to talk to me because my breath really is that bad!* As we left, Nik looked at me and said, "Bro, we are supposed to have the breath of the Holy Spirit, but today you have the breath of the devil." He wasn't wrong. My breath was kicking that day, and I took an L. Even though I was wearing everything right and my hair was on fleek, my bad breath made it impossible to talk to anyone.

Hopefully you have a sense of humor and can laugh at my cringe stories, but more importantly, I want you to understand this: As Christians, we are called to carry an aroma of Jesus everywhere we go. In the Bible, the apostle Paul talked about this: "But I have all things, and abound. I am filled, having received from Epaphroditus the things that came from you, a sweet-smelling fragrance, an acceptable and well-pleasing sacrifice to God" (Phil. 4:18 WEB). Paul experienced the actions of other Christians toward him as a sweet spiritual aroma. The way we live should also be like the breath of Jesus to people.

In order to smell like Christ to those around us, we must *put Him on*. Every day when we wake up, we have to choose to get rid of the hurt feelings, insecurities, and doubts and put on the word of God and praise. As we do that, we will overflow with the sweet smell of Jesus. Trust me, you will catch a lot more victory with Jesus on your side.

DECLARATION:

Father God, thank You for filling me with the Holy Spirit. Everywhere I go today, let me overflow with the sweet smell of Jesus Christ. I want to look more like Jesus today than yesterday. If I have any bad breath or smell in my life, reveal it to me. Give me boldness to share this gospel with the world. I am strong and courageous. I am called. I am chosen.

Scripture Reading: 1 John 4

DAY 51

GOD NEVER LETS GO

...No one will snatch them out of my hand (John 10:28).

On Day 34, I told the story of swimming in a lake in Texas and getting pranked by my friend Zach, who claimed to have seen an alligator in the water. When Zach and I reached the shore, we had to climb onto a little cliff. He got up first and then helped me up. I was thankful he wasn't scrawny so that he could hold up my chunky monkey self. If I had stayed on the shore and said, "Zach, why don't you help me?" but never gave him my hand, it would have been my fault if I got eaten by the gator. To receive help from someone, you have to be willing to be helped. Thankfully, no matter how chunky we may feel spiritually, God is always strong enough to hold us—but we have to let Him. God will not force Himself upon anyone. He wants to be co-workers with us.

The good news is, as soon as we give God something to work with, He doesn't waste any time. Jesus said, "I give them eternal life, and they shall never perish; no one will snatch them out of my hand" (John 10:28). If you ever struggle with thoughts of doubt about your future—*What if lose my salvation? What if I don't do what God tells me to do? What if I never get married?*—know that God has you in His hand.

When you are in His blessing, you don't have to fear. It is not complicated to stay in His hand. All it takes is a willing heart. When you fall, run back into His arms. You may not always be able to count on people, but you can always count on God. You can rest confidently knowing that He has the power, ability, and will to keep you in the right place. Isaiah 49:16 (NLT) says, "See, I have written your name on the palms of my hands." You can always trust that God values you and cares for you. His hand will always be your home. No matter what happens or how you feel, He always welcomes you with open arms. You are family to Him.

DECLARATION:

Father, thank You for holding me in the palm of Your hand. I trust that You are taking care of me. You are taking care of my family. I let go of those worries and cares and choose to stay in Your rest. Your hands will always be strong enough for me. I am loved. I am safe in Your arms. I refuse to accept worry and doubt. I trust the word of God. I will fulfill my destiny. I will walk in the way that You have set before me.

Scripture Reading: John 10

DAY 52

NOW WATCH ME WHIP

For I know the plans I have for you... (Jeremiah 29:11).

I f you have seen those super cringe videos of people try-ing to *whip and nae nae* (it's a new dance), you know that it's almost impossible to watch because it's so cringey. This is because these people are all trying to be something they are not: people with rhythm. If you can embrace the cringe and just enjoy it, that is awesome, but a lot of people will try to be something they aren't and then fear what people think of them. The best way to live life is without the fear of other people's opinions. The Bible teaches us to fear God and not people. My favorite people, the friends I most enjoy being around, are those who are confident and don't need validation from others. When people are confident in who God created them to be, it makes you want to hang around them. You know they won't be expecting and needing too much from you. You can just enjoy hanging out with them.

In the Bible, King Saul made this confession to the prophet Samuel: "I have sinned. I violated the Lord's command and your instructions. I was afraid of the men and so gave in to them" (1 Sam. 15:24). King Saul got so caught up in the opin-ions of people that he lost track of the opinion of God. God's opinion of you is the most important thing in your life. What people think about you will always be temporary, but what God says is what matters most.

When I was in high school, so many people thought I was that "Jesus freak." Recently, I was riding my skateboard in my hometown. I saw some kids I used to go to school with, and we ended up chatting a good bit. They told me that even though they thought I was a little crazy, once they graduated, they realized I was one of the only students who thought for himself. I went against the flow, and they respected that. They even asked me more about what I do now and remarked how much of a blessing it is. It is amazing how people's opinions can change. Their opinions of you will always be temporary, but God's opinion lasts forever. Build your life on God's opinion. When you stand strong on the foundation of the word of God, you will not be moved by feelings or emotions or your reputation. You will be able to be confident and obey God's call, no matter what others think.

DECLARATION:

I am not moved by people's opinions of me. I will build my life on the foundation of God's opinion. What God says about me is what matters most. What God thinks about me is my number-one priority. I reject the fear of people. I will only fear God. God says that I am His child. I am the righteousness of God in Christ Jesus. I am a citizen of heaven. I am called above and not below.

Scripture Reading: Galatians 1

Do Your Job

To reveal his Son in me so that I might preach him among the Gentiles, my immediate response was not to consult any human being (Galatians 1:16).

When I was a scrawny eighth grader, I decided to play JV football. The problem was, I thought I could be coach and quarterback and wide receiver and all the positions on the team. I thought I could help everyone in what they were doing. While I was so caught up in teaching others how to play their positions, I wasn't playing well with my own job. The coach finally chewed me out—"*Do your job,* Gabe! Stop worrying so much about others, and focus on what you need to get done." I didn't know it then, but that was some of the best advice I've ever received.

Jesus said something similar in Matthew 7:1–5:

> *Judge not, that you be not judged. For with what judgment you judge, you will be judged; and with the measure you use, it will be measured back to you. And why do you look at the speck in your brother's eye, but do not consider the plank in your own eye? Or how can you say to your brother, "Let me remove the speck from*

your eye"; and look, a plank is in your own eye? Hypocrite! First remove the plank from your own eye, and then you will see clearly to remove the speck from your brother's eye (NKJV).

God has not called us to police each other. I always laugh when people comment on my videos thinking they will cancel me just because they disagree with what I said. The job God has given you does not include judging others. That is His job and His alone. I will be the first to say that I have made a lot of mistakes in this area. My personality can be so focused on having everything go well that I can try to control people and fix people. But God has not called us to be that way. He has called us to be loving and to allow people to have their own walk with God. We only have one job: to do what God has told *us* to do.

DECLARATION:

Father, thank You for giving me a purpose and a plan. Help me to keep my eyes on the prize. I repent for judging others. I judge myself and say that I am the one who needs to change. Show me the areas of my life that need to change and the times I have spoken wrongly to or about others. You are able to make them stand. Reveal to me how You want me to treat others. Jesus, I love You. Thank You for loving me.

Scripture Reading: Matthew 7

DAY 54

I WANNA BE A COWBOY BABY

Thus also faith by itself, if it does not have
works, is dead (James 2:17 NKJV).

A while back, I saw a guy riding a merry-go-round at a playground and saying, "I wanna be a cowboy baby." Here's the thing: Even though my guy thought he could be a cowboy, he had no chance of actually becoming one, because he was too busy on a playground and not getting any actual work done. He's kinda similar to me, a city boy who moved to Texas and tries to claim he's a cowboy. As much as I may claim to be one, it's all talk.

Unfortunately, we are often like the playground cowboy—more talk than action. And that needs to change. We say we want a strong relationship with God, but we don't spend time with Him. We say we want to know the Bible, but we don't open it. We say we want our family to get saved, but we don't pray for them or love on them. I am exposing myself here, but I am sure I am not the only one who has found himself to be talking too much and not doing enough. We can't have high hopes without a determination to get the job done.

I am not saying you have to work in order to receive salvation, be filled with the Holy Spirit, or be loved by God. Those things are received by faith. But if you want a deeper relationship with God, it is not going to just fall out of the sky. You have to put in a certain amount of time and effort. Nothing in life comes randomly. While God does show us His mercy and grace, He is counting on us to respond in faith and do something with what He has given us. Just as I can't expect to get a girlfriend if I never talk to any women, you can't expect to have a good relationship with God if you don't put in any effort. The good news is, you never have to fear God playing hard to get. He won't play games with you. He loves you and cares for you more than you could ever know. When you take one step toward Him, He will fill the gap.

DECLARATION:

Father, I choose to be honest and real before You. Thank You for giving me the chance to pursue You. I will not make excuses. I choose to draw close to You today, Jesus. I thank You that I am a child of God. I am strong in the Lord and in the power of His might. I am more than a conqueror in Christ. I am not depressed. I am not hopeless. I am full of joy. I am full of light. I am accepted by God. I am not rejected. I am not a worm in the dirt. I am God's beloved.

Scripture Reading: James 4

DAY 55

HAVE NO CHILL

Honor your father and your mother... (Exodus 20:12).

Recently, I went on a trip with my family to Niagara Falls and Thousand Islands in New York state. It was a pretty awesome trip. I am the sort of person who is always exploring and doing crazy stuff, but my parents are a little more serious (maybe a lot more serious), so they are always telling me to chill out. I love running around and talking to strangers and making jokes, but all my life people have told me to "chill out." I love my parents and really appreciate how they raised me, but there were times when they told me to "chill out" on things just because they didn't feel comfortable doing it themselves. It's important to honor your parents and listen to them, but it's also important to have your own faith. If you want to go to church and get closer to God, but your parents tell you to chill, you should know that God will honor you for seeking after Him.

Ultimately, we need to live our lives for God first. If people around us try to pull us down, we still have to keep moving forward. When you are on fire for God, don't listen to anyone who says you need to "calm down" or "you can't keep that energy up." You only have one life; you might as well live it the way God wants you to—*on fire*. It can be challenging living with parents or family members who are different from you. Choose today to honor God and honor them. Before you make decisions, pray about how God wants you to move. He knows the best way forward so that you can honor your parents and family while also staying *on fire* for God.

Honor does not always mean complete obedience. It means that you are willing to hear them and listen to them while submitting to God. The Bible says, "Honor your father and your mother, so that you may live long in the land the Lord your God is giving you" (Exod. 20:12). When you honor and love those who brought you into the world, you are honoring God. Honor simply means to give value and respect to those people. It is also important to honor teachers, bosses, and anyone in authority over you. That being said, always remember to honor God first. That means, if a boss wants you to do something that you know God wouldn't approve of, don't listen to your boss. Remember to put God first, listen to your own heart, and pray about the decision you make.

When I was in high school, teachers would tell me that I *couldn't* talk about God or Jesus while in school. But they were completely wrong. It is actually legal for me to spread the gospel, even in my public high school. They were also wrong because I listen to God first before them. God wants us to spread the gospel, and nothing should stop us, even those in authority (see Acts 5:29). What a waste of time to put people's opinions above God's.

DECLARATION:

Father, thank You for setting me on fire for Jesus. I place Your opinion of me first. Help me to honor my parents and those in authority. Please give me wisdom and knowledge to deal with all the affairs of my life. I want to represent You to the world. Reveal the light of the gospel to my friends and family and city around me. Send laborers across their paths so that they can know You and the power of Jesus Christ.

Scripture Reading: Ephesians 6

CATCHING FEELINGS: YOUR CHOICE

For this reason a man will leave his father and mother and be united to his wife, and the two will become one flesh (Ephesians 5:31).

I t's time to talk about *sex*. Well, kinda sorta. Today we are talking about relationships. But I also want to say that *sex* isn't a bad word. God created sex for marriage. The devil wants to convince the world that sex isn't from God and that you can only have fun when you live in the world. But you don't need to watch bad things or get too close to people to have fun in life. A lot of churches and youth groups preach things like: "Sex is bad. You shouldn't want sex." But I am not here to tell you not to have sex. The truth is, sex actually *is* good—in marriage. When two people have sex, they are joined together. For this reason, God made sex exclusively for marriage; only marriage has the commitment needed to sustain that level of intimacy. It is not wrong to have sexual desire. In fact, it's good to have that desire; God gave it to you. What is wrong is acting on that desire before marriage.

Be patient and trust God to bring the right person across your path. Also, when you have a crush or are interested in someone, make sure you take time to pray about that person. Only God knows who that person truly is on the inside. And focus on being the best person you can be. A lot of people are waiting for "the one" when they aren't "the one" themselves. Grow in your walk with God, work hard in school or your job, and trust God with your desires. Some people say stuff like, "I *couldn't* help myself. I just caught feelings for him/her." The truth is: It will always be your choice how attached you get to someone. That is why it's so important to pray before deciding to date someone. If you are just led by your feelings, you will end up in relationships with people who will get you on the wrong track.

I say this from personal experience. I have found a lot of girls attractive, but after slightly getting to know them, I realized their relationship with God wasn't where it was supposed to be. I'm thankful I didn't just make out with them because they were cute. I'm thankful God helped me have the big picture in mind so that I could remember what's most important—finding someone I'm not just attracted to, but who is also on fire for Jesus.

DECLARATION:

Lord, thank You for creating sex for marriage. I repent if I have committed anything wrong in that area. Thank You for forgiving me and washing me clean. Help me to stay pure before marriage. Help me to keep myself from falling into traps. Give me wisdom to know who to be friends with and who to date. Thank You for leading me today and giving me peace. I will not think or act in lustful ways. I will act on Your word, God.

Scripture Reading: 2 Corinthians 6

DAY 57

NEVER SAY NEVER

He gives strength to the weary... (Isaiah 40:29).

The Bible gives us a life lesson in Isaiah 40:29–31,

He gives strength to the weary and increases the power of the weak. Even youths grow tired and weary, and young men stumble and fall; but those who hope in the Lord will renew their strength. They will soar on wings like eagles; they will run and not grow weary, they will walk and not be faint.

It is easy to look at your current situation and decide you want to quit. *Quitting* is the easy way out. But God did not send His Son, Jesus, to die on the cross and rise again just to have quitters on His team. Imagine if, on the day before Jesus was going to die, He looked at God the Father and was like, "Na, God, this is too much. I'm out." What would have happened? I'll tell you what—we would have all had to pay the price of sin on our own, and we would be due for hell. But thank God Jesus didn't quit; He followed through for me and for you. Now, on the other side of the cross, He offers us the same strength and courage to keep going even when life feels hard and it's tempting to quit.

The passage above promises that God will give us the strength we need. Even when we feel like we are falling, if we put our hope in Jesus, He will renew our strength. He will give us His strength to fight till forever. It's time you make that decision today. Trust God to give you what you need, and choose that you will follow through with everything in life that God tells you to do. I will say, it is good to quit *sin* and to quit living for the world. But don't ever quit doing something that you know God had you start. God doesn't tell us to do stuff without intending that we would finish it. He wants His kingdom completed. And He gives us His strength to keep fighting until His kingdom has come and His will is done on earth as it is in heaven.

DECLARATION:

Jesus, thank You for shedding Your blood on the cross. Thank You for paying the price of sin and death. Thank You for not quitting, but persevering to provide salvation. Create in me a pure heart. I am a fighter and not a quitter. I will finish my course. I will never say never. All things are possible for You, God. When You tell me to do something, I will get the job completed, no matter the cost. Help me to stay focused today and to change the world. Jesus, thank You for living inside me. Greater are You who lives in me than he who is in the world.

Scripture Reading: Isaiah 40

DAY 58

WHAT IS TRULY CONTAGIOUS?

You are the light of the world... (Matthew 5:14).

As I am writing this, in August 2021, the Delta variant of COVID-19 has been all across the news as the most contagious strain yet. My goal here is not to address politics or tell you how to think about COVID. Instead, I want to draw a comparison. The whole world has been impacted by COVID because it is contagious and many prevention measures have been used in many countries. Yet, it is impossible to completely stop the spread of a small and contagious virus. This is a negative contagion, but we have the best and most powerful positive contagion ever—Jesus Christ. His love is way more contagious than any variant of COVID, and He brings life and healing and freedom to our lives.

Infectious diseases like COVID spread from one person to another and then another, and soon enough, whole communities and towns and states and the world are dealing with it. When someone has a disease, if they go out in public, they won't be able to stop it from spreading everywhere. In the same way, God wants us to be contagious with His Son, Jesus Christ. When we go out in public, God doesn't want us to mask our relationship with Him. He wants us to spread His love everywhere we go.

You may be asked to wear a physical mask to follow COVID guidelines, but you should never mask your relationship with Jesus. It is time to spread Jesus Christ everywhere you go. He truly is the antibody to every disease, addiction, depression, and struggle this world has. The Bible says, "You, dear children, are from God and have overcome them, because the one who is in you is greater than the one who is in the world" (1 John 4:4). Jesus Christ, the Son of God, has chosen to make you His home. Think about that for a minute. And Jesus in us is greater than the devil and greater than anything the world can throw at us. Understanding that will change how you live every day. You are His home, and you can spread His love like a powerful contagion. Keep your head up high; the King of kings now lives in you.

DECLARATION:

I am the light of the world. I am a city on a hill. I cannot be hidden. I will not be silent. I am as bold as a lion. In Jesus, nothing is impossible for me. Nothing is impossible for my God. Greater is He who lives inside of me than he who is in the world. God lives inside of me.

Scripture Reading: Matthew 5

DAY 59

SMASH IT UP

Go into all the world, and preach the gospel
to every creature (Mark 16:15 NKJV).

Super Smash Bros is one of my favorite video games. Some people ask me if video games are a sin, and I tell them it is if they play too much and it takes up too much of their time. But in general, video games are not a sin. It's just important to always examine where you spend your time and ask God if He is OK with it. I play Smash Bros a lot with my roommate, and when I first started playing, I would lose every time. I think I went one for fifty in the first few weeks. I didn't understand how he could whoop me so well when I was defending myself and getting space from him. I thought I could win by playing defense—but in Smash Bros, if you only play defense, you will get destroyed. You have to be on the attack to keep the other person from using all of their moves. When you attack, you disarm them and defend yourself as you do it.

This applies to real life as well. The devil wants to put you on the defensive. He wants to get you stuck stewing on your mistakes and thinking about how others have hurt you and said mean things about you. He wants to get you living in shame and feeling condemned for the sins in your past. But I have some good news: We may not know all the moves in

Smash Bros, but we do have the moves to beat the devil. The Bible is the greatest instruction book of all time, and in it, God has given us all the tools we need to be on the attack against the wiles of the devil. Jesus said:

> Go into all the world and preach the gospel to all creation. Whoever believes and is baptized will be saved, but whoever does not believe will be condemned. And these signs will accompany those who believe: In my name they will drive out demons; they will speak in new tongues; they will pick up snakes with their hands; and when they drink deadly poison, it will not hurt them at all; they will place their hands on sick people, and they will get well (Mark 16:15–18).

This gospel that Jesus has called us to spread is constantly on the *attack*. When we get sick, we don't go home and cry about it. Instead, we lay hands on ourselves and pray for healing in Jesus' name. We go after the things that God called us to do. Don't be lazy with your faith. Don't be afraid of what others will think of you. God has your back. Go on the offense today. Google search the scriptures that you need to attack that problem in your life. (Also, don't go punching people because you read this; remember, our fight is with the devil, not people!)

DECLARATION:

Father, I thank You that I am not timid. I am not shy. I am not afraid of the devil. I am not afraid of demons. I believe Your word. There is no fear in me. Show me how to attack the kingdom of darkness and stay on the offense. I will not back down. I will not run away from the fight. I am bold. I am confident. I am strong in faith.

Scripture Reading: Mark 16

GUARD WHAT IS IMPORTANT

Above all else, guard your heart... (Proverbs 4:23).

A couple months ago, I went tubing out on a lake with some friends. All four of us got on a tube while my friend's dad drove us around the lake. Starting out wasn't so bad—until he cranked up the speed. Then I felt like I was hanging on for my life. He took a sharp left turn, and because I was on the right, I knew I was about to fall off. Sure enough, my arms failed me. For a moment—between the tube and the water—I was levitating in the air, but I knew what was about to happen. It felt like I'd hit a brick wall. After smacking the water and coming to the surface, I remembered that I was supposed to shield a particular sensitive male area with my hands, but by then it was too late. I didn't protect myself like I should have, and I ended up paying the price dearly. (Honestly, the stomach aches were the worst side effect.)

The point is, when you have something valuable, you must protect it. This is why people lock the doors to their houses and have a safe to keep their *valuables* protected. The Bible tells us what is most valuable when it says: "Above all else, guard your heart, for everything you do flows from it" (Prov. 4:23). God placed the heart in the center of the body on purpose; it is one of the most important and vital organs that powers the body. Of course, this scripture is not about the physical heart, but the spiritual heart. We each have a spirit, which is our most inner part of who we really are. Just as a hand fits into a glove, so our spirits fit into our bodies. That is why we (our spirits) will keep living even after our physical bodies pass away. The spirit is what powers the physical body, and it lives on after the physical body dies.

When God says to guard your heart, He means you must be very watchful about what you allow into your heart. The Bible also says that the eyes and ears are the doorway to the heart (see Matt. 6:22–23). Having God's standards for what we listen to and watch is very important. I have made a lot of mistakes in this area. I have seen a lot of movies and videos that I should not have watched. I have listened to songs that diluted my heart and filled it with junk. Thank God we can repent, receive forgiveness, and change our ways. *Repenting* does not mean getting forgiveness and then doing the same thing again. *Repenting* means changing your mind and deciding not to go that way again.

Make a decision today that you will be careful about what you allow to get into your ears and eyes. Don't be afraid to make tough decisions to cut out any music, shows, or videos that aren't good for you. I am not going to tell you exactly what stuff to watch or not watch. The Holy Spirit is the one who will guide you in that. But you should always be on guard about what you allow in your life and always follow your conviction (your conscience).

DECLARATION:
Father, I repent for the times when I have not been careful about what I watch and listen to.

I receive Your cleaning. As an act of my will, I release from my soul every unclean, dark, lustful, perverted, or junk-filled thought or idea. My memories are filled with the goodness of God, not evil. My mind is my mind. I will not allow thoughts contrary to the word of God. I cast down every evil imagination. I am strong in Christ and in the power of His might. Lord, give me wisdom to know what to watch and listen to every day.

Scripture Reading: Proverbs 4

WHO WE ARE SIMPING FOR

*For God so **loved** the world that **he gave**...* (John 3:16).

Hopefully the word *simping* is still somewhat trending when you read this. If not, and you have no idea what it means, it basically means that you are caught liking that girl/guy so hard when you are just getting to know them or the feeling isn't yet mutual. (At times, both people could be simping, but typically it's just one-sided.) When you are simping for someone, you often become a little extra and obsessive with your feelings, which becomes off-putting to the other person. A lot of people love joking about it when people are simping hard, because we know they are probably going to get their hearts broken since it may not be mutual. You definitely don't want to be caught simping for a girl/guy who God didn't tell you to be with. Even if God did tell you to be with that person, the best thing you can do is be patient and get His exact wisdom for the next steps. Just because you think someone's *the one* doesn't mean you should rush into anything. The world is not going to end because you can't be with your crush this Friday.

But there is someone you need to be obsessed with every day: Jesus Christ. When you simp for Jesus, you don't have to worry that He won't like you back. He has already made His intentions clear. The Bible says, "For God so loved the world that he gave his one and only Son, that whoever believes in him shall not perish but have eternal life" (John 3:16). Many of us find it easy to obsess over people because we have lost track of our relationship with God. Don't get me wrong: God did create us to love another and to find a meaningful and long-lasting relationship with someone. But God wants us to be so obsessed and in love with Him first, and then we find that special someone while we are chasing *after God*. The best way to find someone to marry is to run after Jesus with all your heart. At some point, you will look beside you and find someone else with the same heart doing the same thing. Make a choice today that you will choose to be addicted to knowing Jesus more. Become obsessed with His goodness.

DECLARATION:

Jesus, help me to keep my eyes on You. I choose not to be distracted. I will be single-minded. Help me to keep my priorities straight. Thank You for giving me great grace. I have been enabled and called to live this life victoriously. Thank You for sending the right friends and people into my life for strong fellowship. I will run after You with all my heart. You find no fault in me. I only do those things that please You. I am Your beloved child, Father God. You are not mad at me. You are not against me. You are for me. Who can be against me when I have You, God, on my side? Nothing is impossible for You.

Scripture Reading: John 3

STAY CONNECTED

Abide in me, as I also remain in you...

(John 15:4).

Think about how fast you scroll through TikTok videos or your Instagram feed. Think about the amount of information you take in every day. You see *a lot* of videos and photos. One of the reasons we spend so much time on social media is that we long for *connection*. When we don't see our friends from school for a long time, we feel out of it. When we lose Wi-Fi, we freak out. Technology, for all of its good, has made us into people who are always trying to get a little dopamine fix from social media interactions. Technology isn't evil, but we must be very careful that we don't allow it to bring us down. We must use it as a tool to spread the gospel and not to get watered down by worldly stuff. (That being said, it's still good to have a bunch of fun, and you can do it the right way without shame or guilt.)

God cares about connection even more than we do. He wants you to make genuine connections with friends—in real life, not just on social media. Some people say, "Gabe, why do I need to go to church if I can get to know God from my house?" My response is: You don't *have to* go to church, but you definitely should *want to* if you want to have a strong community of friends and family who know God. God doesn't want you to live the Christian life alone. A lot of people want more friends, but they are not willing *to be friends* first. You cannot expect people to be nice to you if you are not nice to them.

The best way to make more Christian friends in real life is to make intentional efforts to reach out to people. Go to youth groups and church. Talk about Jesus at your school, and talk to a lot of people. You have nothing to lose. You may feel uncomfortable and awkward at first when you talk to new people, but the more you do it, the easier it will become. Find similarities with others and talk about what they enjoy. Listen to them and remember details. Next time you see them, ask for updates on those details and how their life is going. It won't be long until you find yourself with more than enough Christian friends. Also, don't complain if things aren't working out your way. Instead keep your head up high and trust God. If God guides you to talk to someone or go somewhere, be sure to do it. Miracles will happen when you obey God's voice.

DECLARATION:

Lord, thank You for giving me today. Thank You for sending friends into my life. Show me the places I need to go to make friends. Reveal to me the people You want me to hang around. Help me to influence the people around me instead of being influenced by evil things. Thank You for blessing me with amazing people in my life. I will give You praise and thanks. You are good, and Your mercy endures forever. I am thankful to be alive today. I am excited about my life. I am excited about everything You are doing, God.

Scripture Reading: John 15

DAY 63

DON'T GET DISTRACTED

Fixing our eyes on Jesus...

(Hebrews 12:2).

A while ago, I was really into this girl. She is really cute, and she loves God a lot. I had been friends with her for a while, so I thought it was time for me to shoot my shot. A bunch of us were going to Six Flags, and I was going to talk to her a good bit more and see what might happen. Before we got there, a friend told me to talk to another girl who was roommates with the girl I liked, just to see how the other one would react. This ended up being terrible advice, but I didn't know it until it was too late. I had met this second girl only the week before, yet I started to give her all kinds of attention and found myself talking to her the whole time. I was having a fun time talking with her, but I got distracted and forgot about the mission at hand. I ended giving barely any attention to the girl that I liked because I got distracted with her friend.

In the end, it got pretty complicated. The second girl even asked me what the next steps were, as in, "Are we gonna date or what?" That was when I knew I had caught a fat L. The girl that I wasn't interested in now thought that I wanted her, and the one that I really wanted was left in the dust. The fact that they were roommates definitely didn't make it easier. Thankfully, I was able to communicate to her that we were just friends, and everything ended up being OK. But I could have saved myself a lot of drama if I had stayed focused on my mission.

About distraction, the Bible says:

> *Therefore, since we are surrounded by such a great cloud of witnesses, let us throw off everything that hinders and the sin that so easily entangles. And let us run with perseverance the race marked out for us, fixing our eyes on Jesus, the pioneer and perfecter of faith. For the joy set before him he endured the cross, scorning its shame, and sat down at the right hand of the throne of God* (Hebrews 12:1–2).

Just as I got distracted with the wrong person that day, a lot of times we can get distracted with things that aren't necessarily evil but that take our focus away from God. Just because something seems good and fun doesn't necessarily mean it's from God. We must always be patient and wise before we decide to give our time to a certain person or thing. You may be thinking, *But, Gabe, this girl is just so cute!* Or, *But she goes to church sometimes.* Or, *But he calls himself a Christian.* When something is from God, you will simply have peace about it. You won't have to make excuses for the anxiety and questions you have about a situation. Choose today to follow God's peace, and remind yourself to keep your eyes focused on Jesus and His plan for you. Be quick to turn away from distractions and use wisdom when it comes to the choices you make.

DECLARATION:

I will fulfill my destiny. I will not become distracted. Jesus, I choose to set my eyes on You. You are where my help comes from. Give me wisdom to make the right choices. I have the mind of Christ. I will run my race and finish my course. When I look into the eyes of Jesus, I see who He created me to be. Father, help me to see clearly. Help me to understand what is going on around me.

Scripture Reading: Colossians 1

DAY 64

LET'S TALK ABOUT MONEY

For the love of money is a root of all kinds of evil... (1 Timothy 6:10).

A lot of Christians are very confused about money. They think it is the root of all evil. Some feel weird talking about it in church or in relation to God. Many Christians separate their finances from their walk with God, but this isn't God's will. The Bible actually doesn't say money is the root of all evil, but a root of *all kinds of evil*. (In the King James Version, it does say "root of all evil," but that isn't the best translation of this verse.) In 1 Timothy 6:10, it says, "For the love of money is a root of all kinds of evil. Some people, eager for money, have wandered from the faith and pierced themselves with many griefs." Money is simply a tool here on earth. It is like technology or a car or a house: It can be used for good or for evil. As Christians, we are not called to oppose money; we are to oppose the love of money.

When we say *yes* to Jesus, we are to bring Him into every area of our lives. Because money is part of life, we must put God first in our finances. Some people may say, "I love God, but I don't give to any ministry, because the money I make is my own." If I say I love a girl, but won't pay for her dinner because "that money is my own," do I *really* love her, or is it just words? If we are not willing to sacrifice for the people we love, then it isn't love. True love is always willing to sacrifice. The Bible says, "For God so loved the world *that he gave...*" (John 3:16).

This doesn't mean that you have to give to a certain church. Instead, it means that, as a Christian, you should always pray about your finances and ask God where you should give, whether that is to a person or a ministry or a church. Tithing (giving 10 percent of your income) is an important principle, because it shows that you are willing to place God first in your finances. You don't have to wait until you have an "official" job to start tithing. You can do it now with your allowance or however else you get money. The important thing is that you put God first above your money.

DECLARATION:

Lord, thank You for providing for me—for even the air and food and water that I need every day. God, everything I have, I have because You have given it to me. Everything I have is Yours, God. Help me to continue to seek You first and place Your kingdom as my highest priority. Jesus, I love You. Reveal to me where You want me to give and when You want me to do it. Help my family to understand this principle.

Scripture Reading: Malachi 3

AVOID THE UNNEEDED BEEF

For where envy and self-seeking exist, confusion and every evil thing are there (James 3:16 NKJV).

Today we are going to learn more about beef—not steak, but fighting with people. Just today, my roommates and I were beefing a little bit, so clearly I am learning these lessons with you. Even though God has revealed amazing things about the Bible to me, I still have to practice them every day. I am not perfect; I'm right with you in it. The Bible tells us that God wants us to live a beef-free, or strife-free, life. In James 3:16, it says, "For where envy and self-seeking exist, confusion and every evil thing are there" (NKJV). Here it says *every* evil work is present when we engage in strife, or self-seeking conflict. When we have strife or beef with people, we actually welcome demonic activity into our households. I don't know about you, but I do *not* want the devil getting to my family or friends. We must remember how dangerous it is to allow strife in our lives.

Today, when I was talking with my roommates, we starting getting angry and accusing each other of personal problems. Instead of having a solid conversation, where we figured stuff out, it got into strife. Conflict and disagreement can be good—but when our conversation turns into beef, it is always bad. The good news is, if you are truly walking in

God's love, you can avoid strife at all times. You cannot always avoid other people's feelings or emotions toward you, but when you walk in God's love you will not allow yourself to fall into arguments and division, even if the other person is not walking in love. Sadly, I let myself get into an argument today, and I didn't stop for ten or fifteen minutes.

Arguments, once started, are like a hole that just keeps getting bigger. Be quick to realize your mistakes and walk in forgiveness toward others. When others are angry at you, listen to them and try to understand why they feel that way. Make the needed change, and move on. I'm not saying you should never talk about how you feel. I am saying you need to be honest with people in a loving way and refuse to take things personally. Believe the best of people, even when there isn't much to work with. Think about how you can *bless* those around you instead of looking after your own interests. Even if someone is an "enemy" to you and is attacking you verbally, bless and pray for that person. (If someone is physically attacking you, do what you have to do to stay safe, of course.) If you walk in God's wisdom and love related to conflict, 99 percent of the time you will be able to avoid fights.

DECLARATION:

Father, thank You for showing me how to love others and walk free from strife. I repent for holding unforgiveness or bitterness in my heart. I repent for allowing myself to get into arguments and strife. From this point on, I will walk in Your love toward those around me. I will only create atmospheres of love and peace. I will follow after peace and not strife. Thank You for bringing peace into my family and friends and everywhere I go. Jesus, I love You.

Scripture Reading: 1 Corinthians 13

DAY 66

GET YOUR DRIVER'S LICENSE IN FAITH

In fact, though by this time you ought to be teachers, you need someone to teach you the elementary truths of God's word all over again. You need milk, not solid food (Hebrews 5:12).

The feeling of having your own license to drive is amazing. Without one, you are dependent on your parents to get you anywhere. With one, you are free to go where you want when you want. When I first got my license, as soon as I turned sixteen, I was eager to drive anywhere. I would happily drive to get ketchup from the store or to pick up my little sister. I didn't care where I was going; I was just excited to be free to go without needing to rely on someone else. When you get your license, you transition from relying on others to becoming independent.

In our spiritual walk, God wants us to grow into independence, to have our *own* faith today. When we are little, our parents can believe for us and guide us in God's direction. But the older we get, God wants us to have our own faith so that we can know Him personally. God doesn't want us to rely on other people for our relationship with Him. The Bible says, "In fact, though by this time you ought to be teachers, you need someone to teach you the elementary truths of God's word all over again. You need milk, not solid food" (Heb. 5:12). This verse is talking about the natural way of growing up spiritually.

When you give your life to God, you start as a baby Christian, but you shouldn't stay a baby. You must constantly make the decision to grow spiritually. Physical growth may be automatic, but spiritual growth comes with intentionality. You must eat, exercise, and rest. As you grow in your faith, you will find yourself winning battles that you thought you could never win. When David went out to defeat Goliath, he couldn't take anyone with him. He couldn't lean on help from others. In fact, his family was laughing at him from the sidelines. Thankfully, David knew that *his* covenant with God was more than enough to enable him to defeat Goliath. David didn't rely on other people for his relationship with God; he purposed to grow up spiritually, and because of that, he killed a giant.

The same will be true for us if we pursue our own spiritual growth. A lot of people struggle with God because people in church have let them down. Don't allow yourself to get offended with God just because someone has done something wrong to you. If you keep your faith in God and choose to forgive, those hard times will make you stronger in God, just like David.

DECLARATION:

Lord, thank You for giving me the chance to have my own faith. I have decided that I will grow spiritually. Today, I will feed on Your word and exercise and obey. I will rest in Your finished promises. I will grow up in faith. My faith is my own. I choose to follow You with all my heart. Lord, I love You with all my heart, mind, soul, and strength.

Scripture Reading: Hebrews 5

PARTYING FOR JESUS

Let's have a feast and celebrate (Luke 15:23).

In today's world, whenever we hear about a crazy party, it typically involves drinking, drugs, and fake sex (sex without marriage). Everyone hypes these parties up, but they are temporary and fleshly minded. This is what the world glorifies as fun, but God actually invented parties. Fun was His idea. It's time we, as Christians, start throwing the best parties and having the most fun in the *right* way. We see an example of this in Jesus' story about the prodigal son returning home to his father:

> But the father said to his servants, "Quick! Bring the best robe and put it on him. Put a ring on his finger and sandals on his feet. Bring the fattened calf and kill it. Let's have a feast and celebrate. For this son of mine was dead and is alive again; he was lost and is found." So they began to celebrate (Luke 15:22–24).

Jesus did not have the father say, "Well, we are happy he is back, but parties are from the devil, so we cannot celebrate." Parties are not from the devil; they are from God. God knows how to throw the best party this world has ever seen. In fact, every time a sinner repents, the Bible says the angels and everyone in heaven go wild with rejoicing. The thing about being filled with the Holy Spirit is that you don't need to drink alcohol to have a good time. You don't need to go out and sin to have fun. You can have fun in any setting, because the one who invented fun now lives in you. Everything the world uses for sin is a perversion of something God created.

Don't be so quick to judge those who are living in sin. Sadly, many of them are doing what they are doing because the church has been so boring. Find a church that is fun and passionate in worship. I listen to music with my friends and jump around, and I go two-step country dancing. And on Sunday mornings, I dance even more wildly at the front of the church. My relationship with God is not a side gig. I am passionate about doing a lot of things, but I am always most passionate when it comes to worshiping God. Some people say they "have their own way to worship God," meaning they don't dance or worship in an outwardly enthusiastic way. In response, I ask if they get loud or enthusiastic when watching a football game, or if they will dance at a wedding. If they get passionate at all about anything other than God, they should be even more passionate in worship of God. To be honest, I believe everyone is called to go wild for God. When David danced undignified before the Lord, he didn't do it because he was special (see 2 Sam. 6:14–22). He did it as an example for all of us! It's time we wildly dance for the Lord in worship and praise.

DECLARATION:

Lord, thank You for giving me the chance to have fun in life. Thank You for giving me the chance to worship You in spirit and in truth. I choose to worship You with all of my heart. I will party for You the right way. I have the light of the world living in me. The joy of the Lord is my strength. I will rejoice in the Lord! Oh my soul, rejoice.

Scripture Reading: Luke 15

DAY 68

THIS SPRITE BE
HITTING DIFFERENT

Ask and it will be given to you... (Matthew 7:7).

You know how that first sip of Sprite just has something different about it, especially after you just got done in the heat outside? Last night, I went country dancing with some friends, and afterward I was so exhausted and thirsty. We went to Whataburger, and the first thing I ordered was a large Sprite. I kid you not—I took the first sip while I was talking to a friend, and zoned out for a whole ten seconds. It hit so hard because I was so thirsty. The greater my desire, the greater my refreshment.

When we hunger and thirst for something, we will enjoy it a lot more. The Bible says:

> *Ask and it will be given to you; seek and you will find; knock and the door will be opened to you. For everyone who asks receives; the one who seeks finds; and to the one who knocks, the door will be opened* (Matthew 7:7–8).

Our hunger for God can be stirred up at any time. Our hunger for food can be sped up only through time or exercise, but our hunger for God can be stirred up simply by an act of our will and exercising our faith. If you want to be hungry for God, you can. The good news is, God will give us as much as we are hungry for. Jesus doesn't throw His pearls before swine, meaning that He doesn't waste precious things on people who aren't hungry for them. This is why we must hunger after the things of God. It would be ridiculous to give a three-course dinner to a one-year-old child who isn't hungry for it and doesn't even know how to eat it. Instead, you would give that food to someone who would pay for it and would value it.

God doesn't withhold things *from us* as a punishment or because He doesn't like us. Instead, He hides things *for us* so that we will find them when we are ready for them and can understand and value them. Stir up your hunger for God today. You may say, "But, Gabe, I don't feel hungry for God." Remember, spiritual hunger is a choice. You will be hungry if you exercise your faith and give God thanks for what He has done. Enter His presence today and pray in the Spirit. Worship Him, for He is good, and His mercy endures forever.

DECLARATION:

Lord, give me more hunger for You. I am thirsty for You. I am desperate for You. Thank You for changing my life. Thank You for filling me with the Holy Spirit. Thank You for forgiving all my sin. Thank You for giving me a plan and a purpose. Thank You for revealing Your word to me. Set a fire in my heart that I cannot contain. Show me areas of my life where I haven't valued Your word like I should. I want to make the necessary changes. I want to always honor and value Your things, God. Jesus, I love You.

Scripture Reading: Psalm 63

STOP FOR THE ONE

Let your light shine before others... (Matthew 5:16).

When I was a sophomore in high school, I wanted to get my license right away. In Virginia, you have to take a drivers' school in which you drive around with an instructor for a couple weeks, and then you get your official license. When I was taking the drivers' school, a kid named Cole, who went to a neighboring high school, did it with me. I went to Harrisonburg High School, which was in the city, and Cole went to Broadway High School, which was in the country and more "redneck culture." Because of this, I automatically thought he was pretty weird, and I never really talked to him much. When the drivers' school ended, I didn't think much more about Cole other than to feel bad for him that he went to such a bad school.

A few years later, as I was sitting in the weight room, I saw a breaking news story on my phone. The headline read: "18-Year-Old Cole Rinaca Has Passed Away." I will never forget the feeling of regret I had when I saw that story. The last time I had heard Cole speak, he said he didn't believe in God. While I hope someone told Cole the gospel before he passed away, that might not have happened. I don't blame myself for his death, but I definitely regret not loving him and showing him who God is. Jesus said in Mark 16:15, "Go into all the world and preach the gospel to all creation." That's a responsibility we must take seriously.

I am not telling you this story to make you feel afraid that everyone around you will die soon. But every person on this earth will eventually take their last breath. We don't know when that will be, but we can live today with unconditional love for everyone so that we don't have regrets in the future. And we can intentionally reach out with the gospel. When the right time comes, after we have been showing people that we care and walking in God's light and love, they will start asking questions about God. That's when we should share the gospel with them. It's always good to share the gospel, but it's good to be strategic about it too. If it looks like people really don't want to hear it or they are busy, don't be forceful. Instead, meet them where they are and find some way to help them and *be* a friend. *Be Jesus* to them.

DECLARATION:

Lord, send me into this world to spread Your gospel. Send me. I will go. Give me Your eyes and ears. I want to see people the way You see them. I want to see the world the way You see it. Give me wisdom and the words to say to bring life to others. Let me never become so caught up with myself that I forget my purpose here on earth—to help others. I will be loved. I will walk in the God kind of love. I will care for others just like God cares for me. I will be quick to forgive. I will believe the best of people and situations.

Scripture Reading: Matthew 22

DAY 70

STAY

Whoever acknowledges me before others, I will also acknowledge before my Father in heaven (Matthew 10:32).

It's really tough when a best friend moves away to another state. Often, your whole daily life changes, because you spent so much time hanging out with that person. When we love our friends, we want to be with them at all times. We bring them with us when we go places. If I had a best friend who didn't want to hang out with me much, I'd start to wonder if we were really best friends. We want our friends and boy- or girlfriends to post us on Instagram and bring us into their circle, because true love is willing to show off. True love isn't embarrassed to let the world know.

In the same way, God isn't afraid to show you off. God's not ashamed to call you His child. The question is: Are you ashamed to show off Jesus to the world? Jesus said, "Whoever acknowledges me before others, I will also acknowledge before my Father in heaven. But whoever disowns me before others, I will disown before my Father in heaven" (Matt. 10:32–33). How fake would it be if, after Jesus was publicly shamed and nailed to a cross in front of the world for us, we were afraid to boldly stand up and proclaim His name to our friends and family and city around us? Let's not be fake Christians. Let's stop being ashamed of our Lord and Savior. It may seem like staying quiet about God will make you more popular, but the opinions of people are flaky. If you are willing to give up your salvation for the approval of others, then you are basically just living for other people. Instead of living for other people's approval, we need to live for the opinion of Jesus Christ. We should stay with Him no matter where we go.

Not only will you have God's approval when you stand up for Him publicly, but you will actually get respect from true people who will listen to those who are passionate about what they believe. So many kids in my high school, who weren't Christian, later told me they respected me so much because I stood up for what I believe. People who doubt what they say have never changed the world or had an influence with others. No one wants to listen to someone who isn't sure of anything. Thank God we can be sure that Jesus Christ is Lord. Don't be afraid to stand up for Jesus. It is the wisest way we can live this life.

DECLARATION:

Jesus, I am not ashamed to call You my savior. I will not be moved by the opinions of others. I have not been given the spirit of fear. I have the spirit of power, love, and a sound mind. I am called. I am anointed. I am God's chosen. I am forgiven. I am the righteousness of God in Christ Jesus. I am healed. I am whole. I am free. I will stay with Jesus for the rest of my life. Lord, I will bring You everywhere I go

Scripture Reading: Matthew 10

DAY 71

DON'T JUDGE

Do not judge, or you too will be judged (Matthew 7:1).

A lot of people criticized Kanye West when he started rapping about Jesus. They said things like, "How can he talk about Jesus with his past?" Or, "I don't know if he *really* gave his life to Jesus." It is easy to judge others for their decisions without knowing the full truth. Instead of looking for ways to bring other people down, we should be constantly examining how we can lift each other up. The Bible says, "Who are you to judge someone else's servant? To their own master, servants stand or fall. And they will stand, for the Lord is able to make them stand" (Rom. 14:4). Those who call themselves followers of Jesus are God's servants, and they answer to God. When we think fellow brothers or sisters have made mistakes and we want to judge their actions, it's important to ask ourselves whether they are *our* servants. (The answer is *no*.)

Correction (advice) is different than judgment. Even if you are called to give correction, be sure to say it in love and in the wisdom that God has for you. Have you ever tried to give good advice to family members or friends only to have them bat it down and refuse to listen? Often this happens because we are not careful about *how* we say what we have to say. Even if we have something good and helpful to say, if we use an unkind tone or act superior, it will be hard for that person to receive our advice. Think about how you would want others to treat you and then do likewise. Be thoughtful with the tone and attitude you have with the words you speak. Also remember to only give advice if you have been given an open door. If someone is not close to you or hasn't asked you for your thoughts, be very cautious before you tell them things they should do. Always walk in love and show them how you support them.

DECLARATION:

Lord, I repent for judging others. I repent for complaining and criticizing. Give me wisdom for the words I speak. Set a guard at my mouth so that I speak words of life and not death. Show me ways that I can build others up and not tear them down. Thank You for doing miracles all around me and through me. Thank You for choosing me to spread Your gospel. I will represent You rightly to everyone around me. I am the light of the world. Love lives inside of me. God is love, and He lives in me. Greater is He who lives in me than he who is in the world.

Scripture Reading: Romans 14

SHE A RUNNER. SHE A TRACK STAR

Flee from sexual immorality... (1 Corinthians 6:18).

As I'm writing this, a current viral TikTok sound features videos of people full sprinting in random places, and it's pretty funny. Life gives us a lot of good reasons to run, but today I'm going to give you a *really* good one. The Bible says, "Flee from sexual immorality. All other sins a person commits are outside the body, but whoever sins sexually, sins against their own body" (1 Cor. 6:18). The devil is in a full-on war against our generation to pervert our sexual lives. As we talked about before, sex is a gift that God has given us for marriage. God wants us to be in covenant with our spouse and to enjoy sex in that context only. But through the world and its temptations, the devil seeks to pervert God's plan and get us tripped up in sin that leads us into more darkness.

With the amount of technology we have today, temptation is everywhere. No matter how strong of a Christian you are, you must always be on watch. Do not become prideful and lazy, thinking you are exempt from temptation. Instead, in a humble spirit, choose to pursue God and flee from temptation. It is not a sin to be tempted; it is a sin to act on that temptation. Here's the thing: We can avoid extra and unnecessary temptation if we are careful to stay far away from the line we shouldn't cross. We should become track stars when people slide up in our DMs asking us dirty things. We should become track stars and be quick to run away at any hint of temptation. Don't even get close to the fence, because it is on a very slippery slope.

I have made a lot of mistakes in this area. Far too many times, I have allowed wrong things to come across my phone. I have watched way too many movies and shows that I knew were too close to the fence of temptation. But praise God for the mercy of Jesus. I could get caught up by my mistakes in the past, but instead I have chosen to repent and walk free from it. You can make the same choice today. Don't be ashamed or feel guilty if you have fallen in the area of lust before. Run into God's presence, and He will wash you clean. After you receive forgiveness, ask God for wisdom to avoid those triggers that will lead you down a bad path. God will show you everything you need to know to stay on the right track.

DECLARATION:

Lord, thank You for giving me the ability to stay pure. Thank You for helping me to live free from lust. I am free from addiction. Whom the Son sets free is free indeed. I have no shame or condemnation. I am forgiven. I am loved. Lord, show me the areas of my life where I have gotten too close to sin. Show me what I need to run away from. Jesus, I love You. Jesus, I will run to You today.

Scripture Reading: 1 Corinthians 6

MMM. WHAT YOU SAY

*Whoever **says** to this mountain...* (Mark 11:23 NKJV).

O ver the past few years, my humor has turned so sarcastic that, when I meet people for the first time, they have a hard time understanding what I'm serious about and what I'm joking about. Sarcasm is fun, but I have often made the mistake of taking it too far. Our words are important. As Jesus said:

> *For assuredly, I say to you, whoever says to this mountain, "Be removed and be cast into the sea," and does not doubt in his heart, but believes that those things he says will be done, he will have whatever he says. Therefore I say to you, whatever things you ask when you pray, believe that you receive them, and you will have them* (Mark 11:23–24 NKJV).

When God speaks something into existence, He does not play around. He is always faithful to His word. I'm not saying God doesn't make jokes or act playful, because we know He is fun. But we also know that when He speaks something, He fully believes it will come to pass. This is something we can all work on. If you are like me, you probably say a lot of stuff that you think you might be able to do, but you are really just talking. I want to encourage you today to join with me on the path of accomplishing what you speak. When you always do what you say, you will be quicker to believe your own words, and then your faith will rise. When your faith rises, you will receive everything God wants you to have. We all have room to grow, so don't allow yourself to get down just because you make mistakes and talk too much sometimes. If you have a heart to do what you say, God will honor that.

A lot of Christians wonder why they don't receive from God, and they start blaming Him for things that don't work out. Instead of blaming God or others, let's humble ourselves and work on our words. Life and death are in the power of our words. The Bible says of Abraham, "As it is written: 'I have made you a father of many nations.' He is our father in the sight of God, in whom he believed—the God who gives life to the dead and calls into being things that were not" (Rom. 4:17). Because Abraham believed God, he saw God give life to dead things.

When it comes to the words we speak, it is important that we are honest *and* that we speak the truth of God's word. For example, you may feel sick or depressed or worried, and it is OK to express that, but you must also remember that the Bible says you are healed by Jesus' stripes and that Jesus sets us free indeed. Be sure to always speak biblical truth like you are loading up a clip, and speak it as many times as you need to for your faith to rise. When your faith rises, you will see the victory that God wants you to have.

DECLARATION:

Lord, I thank You for giving me the gift of words. The power of life and death is in my tongue. Put a guard at my mouth so that I only speak words of life. I will do what I say. I will be faithful to my words. God, help me to be more like You. Jesus, I want to look more like You today than I did yesterday. I am strong in faith. I will give glory to God at all times. I am not moved by what I feel or see. I am only moved by the word of God.

Scripture Reading: Romans 4

DAY 74

FOCUS ON THE WIN

*Forgetting what is behind and straining
toward what is ahead* (Philippians 3:13).

Recently, I went bull riding with my friends Zach and Abigail. Even though I grew up in a small city in Virginia, I had never even ridden a horse, not to mention a bull. When we got to the ranch, we watched the first guy get on the bull and start riding. I had never seen anything like it. He was thrown off and trampled from behind. He started coughing up blood and screaming. He could barely breathe. I looked at Zach in shock, seriously reconsidering whether I still wanted to do this. I asked how difficult the bull was, and someone said it was a beginner bull.

As my turn got closer, I asked every question I could think of. I was very curious about what happens when a person falls or makes a mistake. I did not expect the answer I got. A tall, muscular girl who rides bulls weekly looked in my eyes and said, "Stop thinking about what's going to happen when you fall. If you get on this bull thinking about falling, you might as well never ride it." Some people would call what she said stupid, but it was actually exactly what I needed to hear. She got me hyped up, and I ended up riding that bull for more than seven seconds. It was one of the best experiences of my life.

The Bible also talks about the importance of what we focus on. In Philippians 3:13–14, it says,

> Brothers and sisters, I do not consider myself yet to have taken hold of it. But one thing I do: Forgetting what is behind and straining toward what is ahead, I press on toward the goal to win the prize for which God has called me heavenward in Christ Jesus.

God wants you to focus on the victory of Christ Jesus. Do not worry about losing your salvation, being abandoned by God, not graduating, or other fears you may have. Those thoughts of fear and doubt will always try to creep into your mind, but don't give them the time or attention they want. Instead, always remember to focus on what *God says*. When I was riding that bull, if I wanted to stay on, I had to look straight ahead. I couldn't look at the ground. Don't look at your past mistakes and failures or even your present shortcomings and problems. Look right into the word of God and ride out the victory.

DECLARATION:

Jesus, thank You for the victory. I will keep my eyes on the finish line. I will not fear what the devil can do to me. I refuse to worry and stress. I choose instead to enter the rest of God. I will build my life on the word of God. God is my rock and my salvation. God is for me. God has my back. Jesus Christ lives inside of me. I am not afraid of my future. I will run my race and finish my course.

Scripture Reading: Romans 1

MACARONI WITH THE CHICKEN STRIPS

If two of you on earth agree about anything they ask for... (Matthew 18:19).

Macaroni isn't enough just by itself. But when it is combined with chicken strips, then you are on a whole other planet. Having macaroni *and* the chicken strips is like having a best friend. Everything in life changes when you have someone to do it with. This is true in every aspect of life, including our spiritual lives. The good news is, we are never alone, because God is with us. As Jesus said:

> *Again, truly I tell you that if two of you on earth agree about anything they ask for, it will be done for them by my Father in heaven. For where two or three gather in my name, there am I with them* (Matthew 18:19–20).

In life, you may feel like you are just a little lonely macaroni, but God wants you to know that *He* is with you. Stop thinking that you can't do anything special or can't accomplish your dreams. If you were on your own that might be true, but *you aren't alone*. The creator of the universe—the

King of kings and Lord of lords—has chosen to live life with you. The Bible calls us the temple of the Lord (see 1 Cor. 3:16). Think about that for a second. God used to dwell in a human-made temple that was filled with His glory. They had to have extra security and reverence because it was so special to be inside God's temple. Now, God has chosen to make us His home. Because He lives in us, we are never alone. Because He lives in us, we can do great things.

Literally nothing is impossible for the God we serve. Whatever you are facing today—whether it's a tough class or teacher, an annoying friend or sibling, a difficult family issue, or a physical or emotional health struggle—I challenge you to believe that God can handle it. I challenge you to think differently about that situation. Don't just passively let things happen to you. Rise up strong in your faith, knowing that God is with you and believing that in Him you are an overcomer. *God is with you! God is with you! God is with you!*

DECLARATION:

I am not alone. I refuse the spirit of loneliness. Jesus Christ has chosen to live inside of me. I am the temple of the Lord. Nothing is impossible for God. If God is for me, who can be against me? I am more than a conqueror. I am an overcomer. I only take dubs. I already see my victory. Everywhere I go, Jesus goes. Everyone I talk to, Jesus talks to. Everyone I see, Jesus sees. Everyone I hear, Jesus hears. I am the eyes and ears of God on this earth. I am a representation of God to everyone around me. I will be more like Jesus today than I was yesterday. I will walk in love. I will walk in forgiveness. I am led by the Holy Spirit.

Scripture Reading: Matthew 18

BE LED BY THE HOLY SPIRIT, NOT THE DISTRACTIONS

For those who are led by the Spirit of God
are the children of God (Romans 8:14).

In this current season, in which I am believing for God to send me a wife, I have been drawn away to distractions more times than I can count. As much as I want to say I am always led by the Holy Spirit, I have definitely entertained girls who were not very productive with my time. I've allowed myself to be guided by outward attractions instead of the inner voice of the Spirit. About this, the Bible says:

> *For those who are led by the Spirit of God are the children of God. The Spirit you received does not make you slaves, so that you live in fear again; rather, the Spirit you received brought about your adoption to sonship. And by him we cry, "**Abba, Father**." The Spirit himself testifies with our spirit that we are God's children* (Romans 8:14–16).

A lot of Christians want to hear the audible voice of God before they make decisions in life. And that certainly would make decisions easier. But God wants to lead us *by the Holy Spirit*. In fact, the majority of the time, God leads believers through something called the *inward witness*. The best way to describe the inward witness is as the deep-down gut check that we experience throughout our lives. When we received Jesus, the Holy Spirit came and dwelled within us. Now, our spirit (our conscience, which is that gut check and instinct that we have) is joined to the Holy Spirit. Now, when we need to hear God's voice, we can turn inward to that place of our conscience, and the Holy Spirit residing there will help us sense the right direction.

It feels in some ways like a traffic light. Have you ever been about to do something or go somewhere and something just didn't feel right? It's like a red light stopping you. At other times, you may be talking to someone new or about to do something, and you have the opposite feeling: a green light. That is the best way I know how to describe the leading of the Holy Spirit. Tomorrow we will keep grinding on this truth.

DECLARATION:

I am not led by the flesh. I am not led by my eyes. I choose to be led by the Holy Spirit. I will not make decisions just because it feels right. I will make a decision because God is leading me into it. Lord, help me to become more sensitive to the Holy Spirit. Reveal to me any areas of my life that make it harder to hear Your voice. I hear the voice of God. I am a child of God. I am not an orphan. I am not a slave to fear. I am a child of God. I am redeemed.

Scripture Reading: Romans 8

THE ULTIMATE LIFE HACK

My sheep listen to my voice... (John 10:27).

Have you ever clicked on a YouTube life hack video and then spent three hours watching the most clever little tips that make you rethink everything? Those videos are amazing, but they miss the best life hack ever. Being led by the Holy Spirit is the ultimate life hack. He knows every answer to the Geometry test that you have no clue about. He knows which girls and guys should be your friends and which one is *the one*. He knows the best place for you to work. *If you can learn how to be led by the Holy Spirit, you will win in life.* The best news is, no one can accuse you of cheating in life, because the Holy Spirit is the perfect undercover agent. Yesterday, we read in Romans 8:14–16:

> *For those who are led by the Spirit of God are the children of God. The Spirit you received does not make you slaves, so that you live in fear again; rather, the Spirit you received brought about your adoption to sonship. And by him we cry, "Abba, Father." The Spirit himself testifies with our spirit that we are God's children.*

When you choose to be led by the Spirit and not by the flesh, do not get down on yourself if something doesn't work out or you "miss it." It is a learned skill, but the more you practice, the better you'll get. When seeking guidance, it is important to take some time to get away from people and distractions, quiet yourself, and give the Holy Spirit some time to lead and guide. Listen deep down on the inside of your heart and see where you have peace. If you have peace in a certain area, follow that. If something seems slimy and stressful, it is not from God. As you practice following this peace, you will find yourself becoming more and more accurate when it comes to being led by the Spirit. The Bible also says,

> Those who live according to the flesh have their minds set on what the flesh desires; but those who live in accordance with the Spirit have their minds set on what the Spirit desires. The mind governed by the flesh is death, but the mind governed by the Spirit is life and peace (Romans 8:5–6).

The more you fill yourself with fleshly things, the harder it will be to be led by the Spirit. But when you regularly pray in tongues, read the Bible, and worship God, it will be much easier to be led by the Spirit. Remember, that doesn't mean you have to spend long amounts of time in prayer; instead, try to follow Smith Wigglesworth's guideline of never going twenty minutes without prayer.

DECLARATION:

Father, thank You for sending the Holy Spirit to me. I choose to be led by the Spirit of God. I will not be led by the flesh. I will not be led by my feelings. I will not be moved by what I see. I am only moved by the leading of the Holy Spirit. I hear the voice of God. I know when God is leading me. I am not confused. I have a clear mind and clear heart. My heart is pure before God.

Scripture Reading: John 16

DAY 78

GET THOSE GAINS

May God himself, the God of peace, sanctify you through and through. May your whole spirit, soul and body be kept blameless at the coming of our Lord Jesus Christ (1 Thessalonians 5:23).

It may be super cringe to use the word *gains*, because odds are it reminds you of the guys on Instagram with cut off T-shirts and milk jugs filled with water. That being said, the feeling when you gain some good muscle and are in better physical shape than before is awesome. Just as you can improve your physical shape, it is even more important to get gains spiritually. Remember, the Bible describes us as first spirit, then soul, and then body (see 1 Thess. 5:23). The order is important. You are a spirit, you have a soul, and you live in a body. Just as a hand fits into a glove, your spirit fits into your body. This means the spirit is the most important part of you. It helps you connect to God, and it leads the other two parts of you—the soul and body.

When your spirit is strong, your soul and body will reflect that. When your spirit is weak, your soul and body will suffer because of it. A football player knows he won't reach his goals unless he creates a targeted workout regimen. The same is true in your spiritual life. To keep making gains spiritually, follow these three simple disciplines. First, feed on the word of God. Second, put the word into action and exercise your faith, love, and hope. Third, rest in the finished work that Jesus has done for you on the cross.

When growing spiritually, you must also understand your progress. No one starts bench lifting three hundred pounds on the first day at the gym. Even Arnold Schwarzenegger had to start somewhere. The key is to look back at how far you have come and get excited for your future. Seeing that you now have more joy and love and forgiveness than you did before will raise your joy and hope for your future gains. Your faith will rise as you realize how far you have come. As your faith rises, you will go even farther in the Spirit. Make a decision today: You will keep eating up the word of God, putting it into action, and resting in God's strength in and for you. Let's get these gains together.

DECLARATION:

Lord, thank You for how far I have come. Father, thank You for showing me the truth of Your word. Thank You for saving me. Thank You for washing me in Your blood. Thank You for filling me with the Holy Spirit. I am strong in faith. I am not a loser. I am confident of my salvation. I know in whom I have believed. Lord, thank You for being the author and finisher of my faith. You are faithful to hold me. You are faithful to help me grow in you. I will be what You call me to be. I am who You say I am. I am chosen. I am not forsaken.

Scripture Reading: 1 Thessalonians 5

DAY 79

DON'T BE SOUR OR SALTY

Love endures long... (1 Corinthians 13:4 AMPC).

Olivia Rodrigo's album *Sour* may have hit the top of the charts in 2021, but let me tell you, *being sour is* not *the move*. Neither is being salty. Those two words basically mean the same thing here—to be *salty* or *sour* is to remember the wrongs people have done to you and adopt an attitude of bitterness because of it. Maybe a co-worker or classmate looked at you the wrong way or started talking trash about you. Maybe a close friend or boyfriend/girlfriend stabbed you in the back. Whatever happened, the Bible *does not* say it's OK to stay salty. Actually, it says the opposite:

> *Love endures long and is patient and kind; love never is envious nor boils over with jealousy, is not boastful or vainglorious, does not display itself haughtily. It is not conceited (arrogant and inflated with pride); it is not rude (unmannerly) and does not act unbecomingly. Love (God's love in us) does not insist on its own rights or its own way, for it is not self-seeking; it is not touchy or fretful or resentful; it takes no account of the evil done to it [it pays no attention to a suffered wrong]* (1 Corinthians 13:4–5 AMPC).

Pop culture and TikToks may teach us to stir up drama and fight for ourselves, but the Bible says that God is the one who fights for us. Stop trying to get back at people for the wrongs they have done. If you are afraid of being used and you don't want to be soft, then ask the Holy Spirit who you can trust. If someone breaks your trust and you feel betrayed, don't just blame them. Ask yourself whether you were being sensitive to the Holy Spirit in that relationship; perhaps God was speaking to you, telling you to avoid that situation or person. Also remember that people we love and care for are human still and make mistakes. You don't need to feel ashamed, and what the other person did wasn't your fault. But recognizing what happened can help you learn so you can improve in hearing God's warnings as you move forward.

No matter what happens, we must choose to forgive people quickly and forget (let go) their wrongs against us. Pray carefully before you trust friends and let them get close to you. Don't always pull from people, expecting them to move the world for you. Instead, put your expectations in God; He will get the job done no matter who it takes. When we learn to truly forgive and move forward from our hurts, we will be winners in God through our love for one another.

DECLARATION:

I will not be sour. I will not be salty. I will not be bitter. I will walk in the love of God. I will be led by the Spirit of God. Lord, show me the people You have called me to run with. I will be quick to forgive. I choose to release all pain and hurt from my heart. I will believe the best of those around me. My expectation is in God. I will not remember other people's wrongs against me. I will bless those who curse me. I will shine bright with the love of God.

Scripture Reading: 1 Corinthians 13

DAY 80

VALID IN GOD'S SIGHT

...He made us accepted in the Beloved (Ephesians 1:6 NKJV).

As I'm writing, one of the current trends is to call your grandparents *valid* for putting up some cool TikToks and dancing. In today's world, the word *valid* is used only when someone is seen as being cool or acceptable. A month ago, my family was eating some pizza, and my grandma said, "This pizza is bussin'." It was probably the funniest moment I have spent with her. I love it when an older person can relate to teens and young adults. We are used to older people scoffing at us and refusing to relate, so to have my grandma relate felt so amazing. On that day, Grandma was valid in my sight.

About being valid, or accepted, the Bible says:

> *To the praise of the glory of His grace, by which He made us accepted in the Beloved. In Him we have redemption through His blood, the forgiveness of sins, according to the riches of His grace* (Ephesians 1:6–7 NKJV).

In Gen-Z language, you could say that we have been made "valid in God's sight through the blood of Jesus Christ." Grandparents may be valid in our sight, but I am here to tell you that teens and grandparents alike are even more valid in God's eyes. When God sees you, He doesn't think you are far away or too cringeful for Him. He has accepted you, not because you are perfect or never make mistakes or put up cool TikToks, but because He loves you and you claim the blood of Jesus as your redemption. You are valid in God's sight because Jesus Christ is valid. God sees you just like He sees Jesus. Because of what Jesus did, you are forever accepted.

What that means is that you now get to live your life knowing you are valid in God's sight, no matter what others may think. And you can then start to love other people with that same kind of love and acceptance.

DECLARATION:

Father God, thank You for accepting me in the Beloved. I thank You that I am valid in Your sight. I am not defined by my mistakes. I am the righteousness of God in Christ Jesus. I am forgiven. I am loved. God loves me just as much as He loves Jesus. God accepts me because He accepts Jesus. I will focus on God's opinion and not the opinions of people. Jesus, I love You. I choose to love others just like You love me.

Scripture Reading: Ephesians 1

GO FOR THE HOME RUN

And whatever you do, in word or deed, do everything in the name of the Lord Jesus, giving thanks to God the Father through him (Colossians 3:17 ESV).

My biggest regret from the years I played little league baseball is that I was so worried about pleasing my coaches and teammates that I forgot to have fun. I would go up to bat to hit singles and get walks so that I could get on base every time, while my teammates would hit home runs. I played conservatively instead of taking risks, because I thought it would make my coach and teammates happy. But I was missing an important revelation: Even though you might strike out more often when you're going for the home run, it is always worth it because home runs put points on the board. When it comes to the life that we live for Christ, it's time we stop settling for walks and instead hit some home runs. Jesus said:

> Go into all the world and preach the gospel to every creature. He who believes and is baptized will be saved; but he who does not believe will be condemned. And these signs will follow those who believe: In My name they will cast out demons; they will speak with new tongues; they

will take up serpents; and if they drink anything deadly, it will by no means hurt them; they will lay hands on the sick, and they will recover (Mark 16:15–18 NKJV).

Jesus didn't say, "Try to pray for healing and see what God will do," or, "Do your best and then just hope by some long shot that God will hear you." No, Jesus commanded us to have faith in His power and to go for the home run miracles. When you pray for miracles, you have nothing to lose. What's the worst that could happen? Things won't get worse because you prayed. So you might as well go after God with all your heart and swing for the fences. Pray for your friends and family. Pray for those around you in your city and school and the grocery store and streets. Show kindness and listen to them. Be a friend to all. God has your back. Let's get this victory together. Let's love this world so that they can be saved.

DECLARATION:

Lord, thank You for showing me how to pray. I choose to lay down my reputation. I am not moved by the opinions of people. I will not live life just trying to hit singles. I will swing for the fences. God, I will go after You today more than ever before. Jesus, I am thirsty for You. Jesus, I am desperate for You. Use me today to change the world around me. I am strong in faith. I believe miracles will flow from my hands.

Scripture Reading: 2 Timothy 1

WHAT'S YOUR FEED LOOK LIKE?

My son, give attention to my words; incline your ear to my sayings (Proverbs 4:20 NKJV).

I f you have ever used TikTok or YouTube before, you know that the For You page or Recommended page shows you videos that you are more likely to enjoy. A lot of people wonder why they see the videos they do; the primary reason your For You page looks the way it does is because the app tracks what types of videos you usually watch and then shows you similar videos so that you will be more likely to stay in the app and watch for longer periods of time. Where you place your attention determines what you see and what you will be filled with. Similarly, the Bible says:

> *My son, give attention to my words; incline your ear to my sayings. Do not let them depart from your eyes; keep them in the midst of your heart. For they are life to those who find them, and health to all their flesh* (Proverbs 4:20–22 NKJV).

Where we give our attention matters. When we choose to feed on God's word, our hearts will fill up with God's energy—with His peace and hope and comfort. God promises He will never leave us, but that doesn't mean we are forced to stick with Him. So many Christians give more attention to the things of life than they do to God's word. This makes it easy to drift from Him and the life He gives us. When you find yourself feeling exhausted, tired, and alone, run back to the word of God. We must choose to seek Him and His word every day.

The Bible says, "In the beginning was the Word, and the Word was with God, and the Word was God" (John 1:1 NKJV). This means, when you read the word, you are reading Jesus. As you open your Bible today, you are opening up Jesus and His heart for you. If you have a humble heart and seek to know Him more and more every day, you will be transformed into His image. You will start looking more and more like Him every day, and you will be filled with the fruit of His Spirit so that you can thrive in life. Place your attention on the things of God, and He will fill you with His life and power.

DECLARATION:

Lord, thank You for Your word. Your words are life to me. My number-one priority is Your word. Jesus, I want to know You more today. I choose to place my attention on Your eyes. Show me Your glory today. Show me Your goodness. Reveal Your will for my life to me. I will do what You say. I will act according to the word. I am a doer of the word of God. I will accomplish my destiny.

Scripture Reading: 2 Corinthians 3

DAY 83

YOU BELONG WITH ME

You shall love the Lord your God with all your heart, with all your soul, and with all your mind (Matthew 22:37 NKJV).

When you really love someone, you may find your-self wanting that person to belong to you and no one else. In human relationships, that jealous desire for exclusivity can become toxic, because we are not supposed to be God to people. But in our relationship with God, we are called to belong to Him first and foremost. God is actually jealous for us. He doesn't just want half of our hearts. He wants our everything. In the Bible, Moses told the people of Israel, "For you shall worship no other god, for the Lord, whose name is Jealous, is a jealous God" (Exod. 34:14 ESV). Most Christians understand that the Israelites were wrong to worship idols and false gods when they were in the wilderness (and even afterward). But sadly, many of us don't ask what idolatry could look like in our lives. We can end up worshiping idols that we aren't even aware of.

An idol is anything that places itself higher than your relationship with God. If you find yourself spending most of your time and attention on your phone or social media, it has become an idol. If you have a certain love interest who you can't stop thinking about, and that person distracts you from what God has for your life, that person has become an idol. Be quick to identify things or people in your life that have become gods to you. God is jealous to have your whole heart. He wants your undivided attention. He loves with a love that is unlike anything else. His love for you is unconditional. Even in your stubbornness and imperfection, He will always be there.

When you choose to seek Him first and spend time with Him, your joy level will rise, because you were created to serve Him and enjoy His presence. Our lives feel like a puzzle that is finally fitted together when we place Jesus at the center. Be sure to never put God into a box in your life. Instead, let Him fill every area of your life. That way, no matter what you are doing, you will be giving glory to Him and getting closer to Him. There's no better way to live.

DECLARATION:

Father, thank You for loving me with unconditional love. You will never leave me or forsake me. You are jealous for my affection. You are always there for me. You have forgiven me. You have washed me in the blood of Jesus. I am Your child. I am a son/daughter of God. I only do those things that please You. Reveal to me any idols in my life. I place You at the center of it all. I will serve You all the days of my life. I choose to return Your love back to You. Jesus, I love You. Jesus, I love You. Jesus, I love You.

Scripture Reading: 1 Corinthians 8

YOU CAN MISS ME WITH THE GOSSIP

Add fuel to the fire and the blaze goes on. So add an argumentative man to the mix, and you'll keep strife alive (Proverbs 26:21 TPT).

It's funny how everyone in high school says stuff like, "Oh yeah, I hate when people gossip about me. Like, how about they just say it to my face." And then those same people go out and gossip about others. This is because everyone wants to be treated well, but few want to treat others well. Everyone wants to feel loved, yet only some will actually go out and love others. Sadly, I have fallen into gossiping about others more times than I would like to admit. The truth is, the devil is working his butt off to get people to fall into strife and gossip. He knows that if he can get you talking badly about people and creating arguments, your faith will be weak and the kingdom of darkness will grow. Thank God we don't have to fall to his tactics. The Bible says:

> Fire goes out without wood, and quarrels disappear when gossip stops. A quarrelsome person starts fights as easily as hot embers light charcoal or fire lights wood. Rumors are dainty morsels that sink deep into one's heart. Smooth

words may hide a wicked heart, just as a pretty glaze covers a clay pot. People may cover their hatred with pleasant words, but they're deceiving you. They pretend to be kind, but don't believe them. Their hearts are full of many evils (Proverbs 26:20–25 NLT).

We must avoid gossip and backbiting every single day. Be quick to identify times when you feel yourself about to say something rude, and stop yourself. If you have made a mistake and said hurtful things, be quick to repent and apologize to that person. No one is perfect, so when you do make mistakes, it's important to humble yourself before others. If you find out someone else is gossiping about you or saying rude things, forgive them right away, even if they never apologize. That being said, if someone is mean to you behind your back and pulls you down, I do not advise allowing that person to stay a close friend. Your close friends should be those who are your biggest supporters.

The Bible instructs us not to gossip and also not to hold others' wrongs against them. So always forgive *and* let go when people are rude to you. Don't give attention and power to their negative words. Just keep living life and keep your head up high. You are a child of God, and nothing people say can change that.

DECLARATION:

Father, I repent for gossiping and saying rude things about others. Help me to be direct, not backbiting. I repent for complaining and speaking about negative things. I choose to see people from Your perspective. I choose to see situations from Your perspective. I forgive others for the wrongs they have committed. I choose not to remember nasty things said about me. I will keep my head up high and love no matter what. Thank You for defending me so that I don't have to. I will love others unconditionally. I will love others just like You love me, Jesus. Give me wisdom in every situation to act just like You would. I will be more like Jesus today than I was yesterday. Lord, I love You.

Scripture Reading: Proverbs 26

DAY 85

KEEP THE FIRE

I baptize you with water for repentance. But after me comes one who is more powerful than I, whose sandals I am not worthy to carry. He will baptize you with the Holy Spirit and fire (Matthew 3:11).

Once, when I was younger, I spilled a good bit of gasoline right by the shed of my backyard. Most people would simply move on, but I thought I shouldn't leave that gas in the yard. I thought I needed to clean it up, and the only way I could think of to clean it up was to set it on fire. That way, the gas would burn up and disappear. I know, I know—not a good idea. So I ran back into my house, grabbed a lighter, and went back to the shed. Just as I was about to pull the trigger, my mom yelled out to ask me what I was doing. All she saw was that I was about to light a fire near the shed. She didn't even know about the gas on the ground. Thankfully, I stopped and told her, "Mom, I'm just going to get the gas out of the ground, because I spilled it near the shed." She then sternly revealed to me that the shed would be lit on fire if I did that. I still don't know why my fourteen-year-old mind didn't comprehend that until she said it, but thank God she said it before I pulled the trigger. My "amazing" plan that day definitely could have killed me.

The fire I almost started in my backyard would have burned until it had consumed all the available fuel—the gas, the shed, and who knows what else. Fire requires a constant fuel source to maintain its heat. When you give your life to Christ, God ignites a flame in you through the Holy Spirit that He expects you to maintain and grow for the rest of your life. To stay on fire for God, build yourself up in the Holy Spirit through praying in tongues, worshiping God, and reading the word daily. God doesn't want you to have just one or two experiences with Him and then let the flame die out. He wants you to be consistently passionate for Him.

Make a decision today that you will not let the flame of passion for God die out in your heart. Physical fire destroys buildings and communities (and sheds in my backyard), but when you are on fire for God, you will destroy the kingdom of darkness and expand God's kingdom everywhere you go. It is always your choice how passionate you are for God.

DECLARATION:

Father, thank You for setting me on fire for You. Thank You for sending the Holy Spirit into my life. Thank You for the word of God. Thank You for giving me all the tools I need in life to stay on fire for You. I am passionate and excited about everything You are doing in my life. I am excited for the miracles You are working in my family and friends and the city around me. I will be revived everywhere I go. Every place I step into I will release the love of God. Greater are You living in me than he who is in the world. I am on fire for God. I am on fire for Jesus. Nothing can take out the fire that is burning within me. Jesus, burn within me. Give me Your heart for others.

Scripture Reading: Matthew 3

DON'T BE A CRINGE CHRISTIAN

The Son can do nothing by himself... (John 5:19).

Have you ever been in youth group when one of the guys yells out to a girl: "Where's my hug?" Or when the pastor says, "Let's pray," and all the chads run beside the girls to grab their hands—but just for "prayer"? If you haven't witnessed this or done it yourself, count yourself blessed. Don't get me wrong, there is nothing bad about a good hug or prayer. It's just cringe when Christians use these situations to advance their love interests.

The same goes for evangelism. When we share the gospel, it is very important that we don't creep people out. I have seen so many people, when they go street evangelizing, walk up to strangers and immediately start praying for them, talking in a weird tone and over-spiritualizing everything. It is great to pray for strangers, but we always need to make sure we are walking in the wisdom of the Lord. Don't just do things because you see others do it or it looks cool. Check your heart and see what God would have you do. Even Jesus Christ didn't just do things because He thought it was cool. Jesus said:

> *I tell you the truth, the Son can do nothing by himself. He does only what he sees the Father*

doing. Whatever the Father does, the Son also does. For the Father loves the Son and shows him everything he is doing. In fact, the Father will show him how to do even greater works than healing this man. Then you will truly be astonished. For just as the Father gives life to those he raises from the dead, so the Son gives life to anyone he wants (John 5:19–21 NLT).

To spread the gospel, you don't need to preach to everyone. A lot of times, the best way to show God's love is to just *be love,* to have a caring heart for those around you and listen to their words. No one likes someone who just talks incessantly and never lets anyone else speak. When we do that, we don't come across as loving. Show others that you genuinely care about them and their life. When you get a prompting in your heart to pray or share a Bible verse, go ahead. Know that the Holy Spirit is always working through you in every situation as long as you will allow Him.

DECLARATION:

Father, I only want to do the things that You want me to do. I only do those things that please my Father. I only say the things I hear my Father say. I only do the things I see my Father do. I am just like Jesus. I will love like Jesus. I will talk like Jesus. I will pray like Jesus. I will worship like Jesus. I will laugh like Jesus. I will look like Jesus. I am a child of God. I am just like my Father. I have my Father's nature. Lord, thank You for giving me the ability to change the world around me.

I will see miracles today. Lord, I will see You at work today. Let's get this bread.

Scripture Reading: John 5

ANYTHING FOR YOU, JESUS

*But seek first the kingdom of God and his righteousness,
and all these things will be added to you* (Matthew 6:33 ESV).

When I was in middle school, everyone would watch Vines. Vine was like the old TikTok, but only six seconds long. In one really funny loop, a guy was in a bathtub in swim trunks and goggles, and the background music was singing, "Anything for you, Beyoncé." It was so cringe, yet hilarious at the same time. Thank God this devotional is not teaching you how to sing for Beyoncé, because that would be out of pocket. Instead, as Christians, that needs to be our prayer to God: "Anything for You, Jesus."

When you really love someone, you are willing to sacrifice even the most costly items for that person. God so loved us that He was willing to sacrifice His *only Son*. Imagine that for a moment. Imagine if you had only one kid, and he was the center of your world. You worked so hard for him to live a successful life, and he was your most prized possession. Now, imagine sacrificing him for strangers who don't love you or care for you, strangers who actually gossiped about and hurt your family and left you. Do you think you would do it? Most people would say absolutely not, but God did exactly that when He sacrificed Jesus Christ on the cross and placed the sin of the world on Him. Jesus gave it all with *you* on His mind. God sacrificed everything to be with us, yet so many of us still don't want to give up that addiction to lust or music or drugs or toxic friends when He asks us to. How hypocritical is it to receive the love of God and say *yes* to Jesus, but then refuse to sacrifice our fleshly desires because we want to "have fun" and "live it up"?

The truth is, living in sin *is not fun*. Living with addictions and toxic friends and demonic influences is not the move, bro. I challenge you today to sacrifice those idols in your life. Make a decision that if God tells you to do something, you will do it. Don't be ashamed and guilty of your past; instead, just make the right decision today. God loves you so much. I promise you—His plans for your life will always be worth it. It will always be worth it to lay down temporary pleasure for eternal gain.

DECLARATION:

Father, thank You for loving me. Thank You for sacrificing Your only begotten Son for me on the cross. God, You chose to sacrifice everything for me. Thank You for valuing my life more than anyone else does. I am valuable in Your sight. I am precious in Your sight. I am accepted in Your sight. I am not rejected. I choose today to return that love. I will not let that love go to waste. Show me what I need to sacrifice. Show me what I need to change. Show me what I need to give up. I want to burn for You. I want my life to tell the story of Your goodness. I will be a living testimony of the goodness of God. I will not love worldly pleasures. I will not love my flesh. I will not follow after the flesh or the world. Jesus, I will follow You. Jesus, You are everything to me. Let my every choice reflect that.

Scripture Reading: Romans 5

DAY 88

BLESS THE HATERS

Love your enemies... (Luke 6:27 NLT).

The first result that pops up on TikTok when you search my name is: "Is Gabe Poirot a false teacher?" It may seem crazy, but I have to admit, I *love it* when people say hateful things on videos that I make. I'm being completely serious. For one, I find them to be hilariously crafted with more effort than most comments. Sometimes, they are paragraphs full of extensive lists of hateful words that they must have googled to learn. Not only that, but anytime someone is spending attention on my videos, even to comment such things, it helps the videos reach even more people, which results in more salvations and healings. Even though it is sad that many people don't know God and, because of this, attack those who do, I am thankful that I have a chance to pray for them and bless them. Jesus talked about this in Luke 6:27–34:

> *But to you who are willing to listen, I say, love your enemies! Do good to those who hate you. Bless those who curse you. Pray for those who hurt you. If someone slaps you on one cheek, offer the other cheek also. If someone demands your coat, offer your shirt also. Give to anyone who asks; and when things are taken away from*

you, don't try to get them back. Do to others as you would like them to do to you. If you love only those who love you, why should you get credit for that? Even sinners love those who love them! And if you do good only to those who do good to you, why should you get credit? Even sinners do that much! And if you lend money only to those who can repay you, why should you get credit? Even sinners will lend to other sinners for a full return (NLT).

Don't just ignore the haters. Choose instead to bless them and pray for them. Do not take their attacks personally. The Bible says you are blessed when you are persecuted (see Luke 6:22). You don't have to answer to the critics of your life. Instead, just keep moving forward and have a good laugh about it. Nothing frustrates the devil (or your haters) more than someone who finds humor in their attacks. Take joy when people come against you and say hateful things. Pray for them and bless them, because they are being led by demonic influences, and don't hold their words against them. Be like Jesus, who said *while He was being crucified*, "Father, forgive them, for they do not know what they are doing" (Luke 23:34).

DECLARATION:

Lord, I pray for my enemies. I pray for those who have spoken evil against me. I pray for the haters. I choose to bless them. Bless them, Lord. Bless their families. Bless their friends. Help them to find You. Open up their eyes to the light of the gospel. Send laborers across their paths so that they can be saved. Father, forgive them, for they do not know what they are doing. Heal their bodies and restore their souls. Shine bright toward them. Give me wisdom so that I know what to say and how to act around them. Jesus, I love You.

Scripture Reading: Luke 6

YOUR SIN IS NOT WHO YOU ARE

*For the law of the Spirit of life in Christ Jesus has made
me free from the law of sin and death* (Romans 8:2 NKJV).

I am tired of the devil taking over the culture of this generation. We need to stop backing down from people who tell
us how to think according to their "inclusive agenda" that
isn't based on God's values. The truth is, God made us *male
and female.* We can trust God that our biological creation
from the start of our lives was made with purpose. We need
to stop being afraid of saying the truth. Do not be afraid of
being cancelled for standing on God's side.

No matter how you may *feel,* you are who God created
you to be. You should not identify as syrup from Walmart
just because you are feeling sticky one day. Your feelings
and urges do not determine your identity. That is one of the
devil's favorite things to do: He wants you to identify with
your sin and think that is who you are. The devil convinces
people that if they have a thought, they just need to accept
it. But that sin *is not who you are! Know* today that *you are
not your sin.* You are a *child of God.* Do not identify with
those feelings or urges. Instead, identify with the word of
God that calls you free from sin.

It can be tempting, but don't back down from what you
believe because people will label you as non-inclusive. As

Christians, we are called to love people, but *we are not called to love and include sin.* That being said, this is not an excuse to judge other people. Apply this to your own walk with God. If you know people who are living in sexual sin, pray for them and bless them. If they are Christians, you have a good friendship with them, and they have a heart for God, then you should definitely talk to them about what the Bible says on this issue. But be wise with your words and don't be forceful; just point out the scripture once and let them choose. If people are not Christians and are living in sexual sin, don't criticize and condemn them. Because they don't know God yet, they have no reason to not live in sin. Just love them and lead them to Jesus. You cannot clean fish before you catch them. So don't try to make people better; just lead them to Jesus, and He will do the work in their lives.

DECLARATION:

Father, thank You for making me a new creation in Christ Jesus. The old is past and all things have become brand new. My past is gone. I am not a slave to sin. I am not a slave to fear. I am a child of God. Sin is not who I am. Temptation is not who I am. Feelings are not who I am. Bad and evil thoughts are not who I am. I am the righteousness of God in Christ Jesus. I am born again. I am just like my Father God. I am who God says I am. I am who God created me to be. I will not be confused. I will not be bound by demonic oppression. I will not be led by the lust of the flesh. I will be led by the Spirit of God. I find my identity in Christ Jesus alone. I am bought by the blood of Jesus. I am free from sin. I am free from shame. I am free from guilt.

Scripture Reading: Mark 10

DAY 90

SQUAD UP

[He] has made us kings and priests to His
God and Father... (Revelation 1:6 NKJV).

love the imagery of an army—a group of people joining up with a common purpose. That's how I feel when going somewhere with a group of friends. It feels so awesome to squad up and influence everyone around us. But this isn't just for our fun times with friends. God has drafted us into His squad. In school, we often see exclusive cliques who won't let people join them, but God's army in not exclusive. All are welcome, no matter their gender, skin color, ethnicity, status, history, and so forth.

It doesn't matter how many times you have failed. It doesn't matter how "good" of a Christian you are or how attractive you are. God has chosen you, and He has an amazing destiny for you. Stop thinking of yourself as lowly. You are not a worm in the dirt. You are part of God's squad now. The King of kings and Lord of lords has chosen *you*! Let that sink in for a moment. The creator of the universe, the Alpha and Omega, the beginning and the end, has specifically called you to squad up and win this world back to Him. Let your every decision and thought reflect this reality. Change your mind to see yourself as part of God's inner circle.

Have confidence, because God has your back. Wake up every day hungry to see souls saved and lives impacted for the kingdom of God. Don't be soft. Don't be shy or timid. Don't be afraid to put yourself out there and talk to people. Put down the fear of people and pick up the armor of God. We don't have time to waste. Jesus is coming back soon for a squad that is ready for Him (see Rev. 22:12). Get ready, because Jesus is almost here. Kick the sin out of your life, and welcome in God's glory and fire. *You are built different, because Jesus Christ now lives in you. Let's go!*

DECLARATION:

Father God, thank You for drafting me into Your army. I am chosen for such a time as this. I will fulfill my destiny. I will do everything You tell me to do. I am a soldier in the army of the Lord. I am part of God's squad. I will not back down. I will never quit. I will never give in to the devil's tactics. I will not be moved by what I see or feel. I am a fighter. I am a winner. I am free from sin. I am a new creation in Christ Jesus. I will walk in love. I will be led by the Spirit of God. I am on fire for God. I am full of the Holy Spirit. The greater one lives inside of me. Greater is He who lives in me than he who is in the world. Jesus Christ now lives in me. I am built different, because Jesus is built different. Jesus, I love You. I will follow You all the days of my life.

Scripture Reading: 2 Timothy 2

YOU DID IT!
YOU FINISHED!

Continue to read your Bible, praise God, pray in tongues, and hang out with Jesus every day. Go to a strong church and make Christian friends. Always love God, love others, *and live life with joy!*

ABOUT THE AUTHOR

Bold. Joyful. Hilarious. Passionate.

These are just some of the words that describe social media personality Gabe Poirot. Poirot is a speaker, content creator, consultant, and author. In 2020, he started preaching the gospel on TikTok, YouTube, and Instagram to an audience that has grown to a combined 1.9 million followers and more than 280 million cumulative views.

Known by his passionate and joyful walk with Jesus, Gabe is committed to bringing the good news of God's power and love to this next generation.

Equipping Believers to Walk in the Abundant Life
John 10:10b

Connect with us for fresh content and news about forthcoming books from your favorite authors...

 Facebook @ HarrisonHousePublishers

 Instagram @ HarrisonHousePublishing

 www.harrisonhouse.com